10/85   D 208445   £19-20

7

★ LADIES OF THE EVENING:

Women Characters of Prime-Time Television

by
DIANA M. MEEHAN

The Scarecrow Press, Inc.
Metuchen, N.J., & London
1983

Library of Congress Cataloging in Publication Data

Meehan, Diana M., 1943–
   Ladies of the evening.

   Bibliography: p.
   Includes index.
   1. Women in television--United States. I. Title.
PN1992.8.W65M43 1983   791.43'09'09352042   83–8702
ISBN 0–8108–1634–2

FOR GARY

Television has been around now for more than thirty years, presenting a variety of characters, images of people, and ways of behaving to the American viewing public. There has been considerable speculation and argument about the kinds of messages television has presented to viewers from 1950 to the present. Feminists, for example, who were concerned with questions relating to sex role behaviors and attitudes about women and men, expressed anger about television's portrayals of female images and roles. They questioned the accuracy of the portrayals and the potential effects on the television audience. As a feminist, I share their concern, and as a media researcher, I share their interest. Before assessing the accuracy of the portrayals or the likely impact upon viewers, however, it is necessary to have specific and accurate descriptions of television characters and behaviors and some index of any change over time. Toward this end I began five years ago to describe and interpret some of the characters that we had seen on our television screens from 1950 to the present.

I concentrated on women characters. Not only are women frequent viewers but women are underrepresented on television so the medium's presentations of this sex are particularly potent. They are reflections of women's lives, implicit endorsements of beliefs and values about women in a very popular forum.

Having determined the subject of the study I chose an eclectic approach to research it. There are several approaches to an analysis of female television characters, among which are the quantitative, the interpretive, and the comparative. Each has advantages and shortcomings for evaluating television's portrayal of women.   At one point or another, I tried them all.

The quantitative approach, a scientific method based on numbering items or events, offered precision.   By counting the numbers of female characters or female heroes, or the numbers of times that situation comedy jokes were at the expense of a female or that dramatic acts of violence were committed by women or against women, I reached some conclusions about television's view of women.   Social scientists who research media effects have found that the mere presence or absence of images has an effect on viewers, therefore documenting sheer quantities of images was useful.

I decided that the quantitative method by itself was inadequate, however, for answering questions about the attitudes and values expressed about women in the television portrayals. Although sheer quantity is important, the context of the story was clearly a factor in either positive or negative evaluations. The manner in which female characters were presented, and the reality and intensity of these portrayals, were better assessed by an interpretive approach, which allowed a consideration of the characters in the context of the stories.   Thus, I prepared descriptive and analytic notes (field notes) evaluating the characters as if they were real people much the way anthropologists and sociologists analyze people and settings.

With the interpretive approach, questions about women characters' power and powerlessness, vulnerability and strength could be addressed.   I categorized behaviors that reflected or failed to reflect sex stereotypes, those that depicted women in recurring roles, and dialogue that was humorous or about women or about the female characters themselves.   I considered how female characters interacted with other characters in work, community, and interpersonal relationships.

Considering female characters as real people led to questions about the representativeness of television's portrayals of women, that is, how female characters compared with the female population.   I therefore turned to the comparative approach and combined information from both quantitative and interpretive media research and the results of demographic studies of the actual population to answer some of these questions.

Due to time restrictions (I allowed two years for the reviewing of selected programs and one year for writing the analysis from field notes), the programs selected for description and analysis were limited. I chose episodic formats because they had consistent casts of characters, who were approximations of real people. I selected only top-rated network shows since their popularity suggested that they were more representative of American tastes (and therefore American values and beliefs) than local, short-lived, or less popular programs.

From an exhaustive list of network episodic series aired within the period from 1950 to 1980, I chose five series to represent programming of each five-year period; two situation comedies and two episodic dramas were selected for each period, based on popularity and similarity of format. In addition, one or more shows for each five-year period were previewed to provide the perspective of a unique format, a female lead, or unusual setting. Thirty-three shows in all are represented: 1950-1955--Big Town, Dragnet, I Love Lucy, and Life of Riley; 1955-1960--Gunsmoke, Maverick, The Adventures of Ozzie and Harriet, The Rifleman, Decoy, and The Ann Sothern Show; 1960-1965--Bonanza, Dr. Kildare, Beverly Hillbillies, Dick Van Dyke, and Big Valley; 1965-1970--Ironside, Mission Impossible, Bewitched, Family Affair, and The Ghost and Mrs. Muir, and That Girl; 1970-1975--Marcus Welby, M.D., Medical Center, Mannix, All in the Family, The Mary Tyler Moore Show, Maude, and Streets of San Francisco; 1975-1980--Policewoman, Charlie's Angels, Laverne and Shirley, M*A*S*H, and Hart to Hart.

To enhance accurate description of the selected programs I videotaped episodes or previewed episodes from film archives and supplemented my notes with scripts whenever available.

Two episodes of each program were randomly selected from all available episodes. Other arbitrarily selected episodes of the sample programs were viewed in addition to the videotaped or filmed programs to provide additional information.

All of the procedures described above contributed to my own analysis of the characters and images presented in television programs. Besides my own analysis, I sought the research and opinion of other writers for their interpretations

ix

of both television programs and the times in which they aired. I studied newspaper stories and magazine advertisements and articles as an index to the times, the context in which certain shows were popular. In addition to reading random selections from Newsweek, The New York Times, and Ladies' Home Journal, I reviewed scientific accounts of events of each period. Studies by sociologists, historians, and communicologists regarding social and historical trends of each five-year period were helpful by providing accounts of actual events with which to compare television versions. Circumstances of working women, as reviewed in sociological surveys, for example, were comparable with the medium's representation of working women. I also referred to the findings of other media researchers and television analysts where their observations seemed relevant.

Finally, I conducted interviews with fifteen television writers in the last two years of the study because writers were primary creators of the characters and the events depicted on the television screen. Their insights and observations verified some of my conclusions and suggested new ones sometimes. In addition to interviews, I was permitted to sit in on writing sessions for one week by the writer-producers of The Bob Newhart Show. More than once I got a hot meal as well as a collection of treasured gags and anecdotes about the competition or about the early days of television.

Five years have passed since I started this research. At times the conclusions I was reaching were disheartening and depressing. The writing was tiring and frustrating but sometimes exhilarating. It hasn't been boring, anyway.

D. M. M.

★ ACKNOWLEDGMENTS

First and foremost are Gary and Shana, who shared the journey and urged me on.

My debt to my academic advisers--Ken Sereno, Billie Wahlstrom, Carol Warren, Bob Smith, and most especially, Ed Bodaken--began seven years ago. Their counsel and their patience were invaluable even though I sometimes failed to heed the former and sorely tried the latter.

Those who agreed to be interviewed provided some of the research underpinnings of this book. They are Bob Schiller and Bob Weiskopf, Madelyn Davis and Bob Carroll, Lynne and Gordon Farr, Lloyd Garver, Patricia Jones and Donald Reiker, Ed. Weinberger, Michael Zinberg, Diana Gould, and Susan Seeger. Allan Burns, Michele Gallery, and Seth Freeman provided "deep background" about the television process and some of the characters they have created.

I also appreciate the efforts of friends who offered advice, criticism, and sometimes a kitchen to cry in: Allen Weiner, Susan Shimanoff, Janet Weathers, Keven Bellows, Jim Preminger, Barbara Hooper, and Dick Levinson. My parents, Jack and Brenda Meehan, are in this category, too.

In the preparation of the manuscript I had the able assistance of Phyllis Mitchell as typist. Phyllis also checked names in TV Guide, clipped relevant reviews, and offered the observations of a prime-time fan.

Finally, as an employed mother I have a special category of thanks to the individuals and organizations that aided and abetted my "outside" life: UBU Productions, especially Dianne Edwards; Lincoln Pre-School and St. Augustine by the Sea; Louise's Kitchen, the Coral Beach Cantina, and Anna Maria's La Tratoria on Wilshire Boulevard; Gloria Lopez and Garcia's Gardening Service; and for emergency caretaking and nurturing, Uncle Tom and Aunt Lena. I am grateful to you all.

PART I

★

INTRODUCTION

One of the predominant experiences connecting Americans is prime-time television. The television program that we watched last night and talked about today unites us to our fellows, viewers and non-viewers alike, who know who shot J.R. and who caught Joe Montana's pass in Superbowl XVI. The television shows that we saw long, long ago unite us, as well. Those who saw television's early seasons shared Lucy's birth of Little Ricky, a national experience as connective and compelling as the previous decade's Fireside Chats on radio. Those who watched Ed Sullivan every Sunday night shared an American event which was in many families as much a ritual as morning coffee.

Each decade since the fifties has had its Lucys and Ed Sullivans, its media figures who appeal and who make us laugh, hope, want. They color our personal visions, especially in our youth. A boy from Brooklyn who grew up watching Ozzie and Harriet and Leave It to Beaver said he always wanted to misbehave (at home) and be sent upstairs to his room as Ricky Nelson and Beaver Cleaver were, but neither he nor anyone else he knew had an upstairs, let alone his own room. He is an adult now, the father of a ten-year-old and when he sends her upstairs to her room his momentary frustration is always mixed with a certain satisfaction that comes from living an image from his past, an image shared by many in his generation.

These images and heroes are important for they link us to other Americans and they also give us ideas about who we are and what's important. Our television fare conveys attitudes, beliefs, and values about the world in which we live, even if broadcasters don't intend it. Although these

3

ideas are incidental to the humor or the pathos of the story,
they are not unimportant. As psychologists and psychiatrists
have long insisted, ideas and values that no one intended us
to learn can be the forces that shape our lives. [1]

⌐ Situation comedies (known as "sit-coms") and nighttime
soaps provide viewers with ideas and values; moreover, there
is considerable evidence that such television content serves
as a model for audience members' behavior as well. To an
important degree, we become what we have seen. Children,
especially, identify with television models, incorporating traits
and behaviors of favorite characters into their own systems
of expression.⌐ Sometimes, as that boy from Brooklyn can
verify, it is years later that the behavior appears. However,
it is not just children who model their behaviors after television actions; we older viewers, too, learn ways of interacting,
coping, and communicating from media characters. [2]

Television characters convey information about roles
(that is, how to act in such and such situation), some of
which is quite useless to most of us--how to act as a dance
hall floozie and how to be a police snitch, for two examples.
Yet some roles conveyed by the fantasy characters we see
are the commonplace ones of spouse, parent, employee,
neighbor. Most social scientists who have studied the subject argue that viewers learn what's appropriate in these
roles from media models as well as from real ones. [3] Lucy
and Ricky and "the Beav" aren't the only ones who teach us
roles, but for many of us they were among our models.

Furthermore, our media models tell us what other
people are supposed to do, too. Social science researchers
usually call it role expectation, the viewers' anticipation of
how others will behave within the role framework. Our expectations for mates, mothers, manicurists--even robbers,
thieves, and whores--are to some extent affected by their
media images. Thus, viewers, especially frequent viewers,
evaluate the behavior of others as appropriate or inappropriate compared with television models, and life and its television versions become even more interrelated.

⌐ Television images eventually affect even the non-
audience folks who, after all, live in the same society with
those who watch.⌐ Presumably they learn to respond appropriately when the heroes and events of the television arena
are discussed and dissected by those around them. Both
football widows and the parents of pre-schoolers learn names

of superheroes (sports and cartoon, respectively) whom they
may know only by hearsay but who are the objects of their
loved ones' attention.

Nor are non-viewers immune from television's images
in other settings.   They can find them everywhere: the television figures who appear in other media, such as magazines
and films; the faces and bodies of prime-time and day-time
shows, who decorate products from shoes to shampoo on bill-
boards, store displays, and wrappers; the expressions and
catchwords that gain popular currency from public exposure
on prime-time air. *Exposure to any media means you'll come into
contact with gendered characters from TV.*
The influence of other institutions (the family, the
school, the church), which we might expect to counter or bal-
ance the images depicted in television content, is itself subject to the medium's influence.   Family conversations, school-
room discussions, and even Sunday sermons are peppered
with television expressions and characters and events.   Children and adults discuss prime-time plots and televised sporting events at work, at play, and at home.

The pervasiveness of media images contribute to making them American idiom and lore.   They are the coins of
our experience as Americans.   The expressions, the characters, and events--the birth of Little Ricky, the shooting of
J. R. --serve to link us with others of our sex and generation
who have shared that television experience.

The television experience of the past thirty years was
almost a laboratory situation so dominant were the networks,
so pervasive the images they presented.   An entire nation of
viewers chose one of three nighttime offerings, absorbing and
sometimes endorsing what prime time presented.   The tape
and film of those television seasons are an index to the values
and ideas of the era.

Prime-time television's era of dominance is no more.
Cable programming competes with network offerings and video
games challenge both of them for viewer attention.   The next
generation will have a wider array of video experiences from
which to choose--heroes by video game-manufacturer Atari
and by Cable News Network president, Ted Turner, in addition to prime time's contenders.

The future's heroes will be set in a world that reflects
the ideas and ideals of the times, yet they will be cut from

the mold of the past.   Characters from the movies Star
Wars and Raiders of the Lost Ark owe their traits and circumstances to earlier characters in other genres.   So, too,
have television characters evolved from print, film, and
radio figures who preceded them: the Lone Ranger, George
Burns and Gracie Allen, Dragnet's Joe Friday, Batman and
Wonder Woman, the M*A*S*H crew, to name a few.   Like
popular characters of previous decades, the ones of seasons
to come will be molded on the heroes and villains of the
past. [4]

    Thus, it is important for us to study television's past
heroes.   They are the antecedents of fantasy heroes of the
future.   In addition, the images and roles presented on fantasy formats have real life consequences since they provide
models for behavior and ideas and expectations, however
faulty, about the way the world works.   Prime-time television is a key to our common past as Americans, as well as
a wealth of clues to the future--our own future and that of
video characters we can expect to see there.

    Over the course of the thirty years that prime time
has predominated, we have been privy to aspects and episodes of thousands of characters.   Researchers of this vast
video landscape have focused on the male characters who
dominated the period.   Yet we have seen an abundant array
of female figures, models for our expectations of wives,
lovers, mothers, sisters, victims, and friends.   What kind
of women are these ladies of the evening whom we've had
in our homes for thirty years?   To answer that question is
the purpose of the succeeding chapters.

PART II

★

BEHIND CENTER STAGE

2 ★ WHAT THE CREATORS THINK OF
THE PAGEANT OF PRIME TIME

To those of us on the home side of the tube, television can
be a fantasy world, a glamour machine, an ogre, or a drug.
To the people on the other side where those horrible/won-
derful creations begin, it is a business.   Television is in
the custody of advertising, sales and profit-minded business
people who view the ideas, ideals, and events depicted on
the screen as secondary chracteristics of their business.
Their business is developing and selling a product, but the
product is not entertainment, as we viewers might expect,
but audience.   The product is us.[1]

        "What network people want," a producer said off-the-
record, "is to keep their jobs and to do what they have to
[to] deliver an audience to the advertisers."   A network
vice-president, Al Schneider, echoed the producer's conclusion when he told another interviewer, "It seems to me, in
order to exist as a commercial broadcaster, the mandate
quite properly is to attract most of the time of the audience...."[2] "Capturing an audience," as television writers
Levinson and Link observed, "is an infuriatingly inexact
science."[3] To minimize mistakes and avoid personal blame,
television's professional buyers exercise a complicated series of measures designed to determine what lure will succeed.   Network representatives secure an idea, identified
as a "premise," and subsequently they test the concept, the
script, and the pilot; they also interview and evaluate the
cast members and they appraise the director, crew, and
choice of locale.   These procedures, embellished with
lunches, meetings, and numerous notes at several stages of
the process, are designed to make the creation of fantasy
feel more like a business.

The creators and promoters of television are comfortable in the business of being a business. Their jargon
is layered with terms relevant to production and profit-
sharing. They refer to the broadcast system as The Industry or The Business and discuss "taking" meetings and making deals. In the course of their average workday, media
people sell time, buy ideas, and can laughter. Little wonder if they come to have less than a dewy-eyed view of
their product: the audience members who are counted like
sheep, like assembly-line packages every night in every
major city. However, such conclusions are premature,
without the background of the historical context in which
they developed.

BACKGROUND TO THE STORY

The present broadcast system came to be a business largely
as a result of the Communications Act of 1934, which defined the basis on which present regulations and practices
are operated. This act, largely a rephrasing of a 1927 act,
put television in the hands of free enterprise. Nevertheless,
television remained little more than a technological curiosity
for the next fifteen years. Then in 1951, the coaxial cable
was laid, enabling viewers from coast to coast to simultaneously participate in a single video event. Network television as we know it was born.

Programming in the early days was dominated by
variety, dramatic anthology, game shows, and sports presentations. In the 1950-1951 season, however, the trend
for future prime-time programming was glimpsed in the top-
rated lineup of ten shows, which included a Western, a spy-
crime show, and a situation comedy. Each of the three formats had originated in another medium, but with repeated
interpretations in prime-time programming, it became a distinctive television genre.

Episodic television, defined as series of shows about
a recurring cast of characters broadcast over a season's
time, featured both dramatic and comic genres. Comic series were distinguished by the consistent use of humor, although later the distinction blurred, as in episodes of Lou
Grant and M*A*S*H. In dramatic programs the definitive
characteristic of the series was the presentation, exploration, and resolution of conflict. Dramatic series included
Westerns, crime and spy formats, and professional drama
among their offerings.

The earliest successful dramatic genre on episodic
television was spy-crime, a chronicle of the action-bound
adventures of a heroic crusader dedicated to law, justice,
and the propagation of a parochialism identified as American philosophy.   I Cover Times Square, Martin Kane, Front
Page Detective, Rocky King, Inside Detective, and Big Town,
followed closely by Dragnet and others, concerned the mar-
shalling of good against evil in the fight against crime and
subversion.   These shows were always set in a big city.
"This is the city," Dragnet's hero began each week.   It
gave a certain malevolence to the urban setting, as if crime
and corruption were unknown in the rural landscape.   Little
character development or introspection occurred as the urban hero wrestled with opponents of his view of the universe,
and in this respect the show resembled the early Westerns
which premiered the same season.

The Western, a particularly American phenomenon,
came from literature, radio, and film, but in television its
colorful dialogue, characters, and convention were crystal-
lized to epic form.   The popularity of such children's programs as The Lone Ranger and Hopalong Cassidy convinced
filmmakers to enter the television business, bringing cine-
matic expertise and thematic sophistication to their efforts.
And the adult Western was born.

Unlike their predecessors aimed primarily at children, the adult Westerns--Gunsmoke, The Life and Legend
of Wyatt Earp, Cheyenne, and the fifty-three others which
appeared in that first decade--were programmed at prime
time.   Other than frontier locale, what defined these shows
was violent action presented as barroom brawls, runaway
horses, showdowns, and shootouts.   At times they were as
moralistic and simplistic as the juvenile versions but despite the bloodshed and moral superiority of the hero, they
sometimes addressed more complicated issues of individual
versus community rights and the dilemma of conflicting but
appealing philosophies.   When Matt Dillon said, "That's
what worries me, Kitty," what worried him was more likely to be the irruption of mob reaction or the intrusion of
moneyed men from the East rather than ambush by Indians.

The ethnical and philosophical issues only partly articulated in prime-time Westerns were the primary staple
of professional dramas which burst on the screen six years
after the Western boom.   Epitomized by The Defenders and
Dr. Kildare, the drama series considered moral aspects of

the individual's confrontation with social issues, such as
criminal behavior, insanity, abortion, euthanasia, and even
bureaucratic ineptitude at the individual's expense. The
heroes of these purposive parables were young professionals
--brilliant, rebellious, sometimes abrasive students of
humanity--apprenticed to a mentor who cautioned and advised the young doctor, lawyer, teacher, psychiatrist, or
priest.

Concurrent with all of these dramas and continuing
into the present prime-time season were the situation comedies.   From the beginning of network television, situation
comedy has been an episodic form which has captured ratings by presenting comic versions of credible people struggling with the everyday.   From the first "Hi, honey, I'm
home" to the last chuckle of the laughtrack, episodes dramatized characters struggling with personal problems, marital conflict, economic and domestic troubles.

Initially, situation comedies were always set in the
home.   Madelyn Davis, who wrote I Love Lucy with partner
Bob Carroll, explained the attraction of the domestic scene:
"You're starting from a base the people understand ... a
basic situation that everyone knows."4   Another successful
writer, Bob Weiskopf of Maude and All in the Family,
agreed with that: "The household is the arena that we can
all relate to.   We know what it's like when the sink stops
up."5

Television's comic genre matured and moved into the
workplace, but the characters continued to treat each other
like family.   The boss was paternal, the primary (or sole)
female figure was often maternal and their cohorts acted
like kids or neighbors.   It was a formula that fit even innovative situation comedies of recent seasons, such as Barney Miller, One Day at a Time, M*A*S*H, and Alice.
Writer Bob Carroll said, "On Alice Mel is almost the
father ... on TV people want to tune in and see what they
know: people with problems, family relationships."6

Within the framework of family relationships, situation comedy grew to consider a wide range of topics eventually including homosexuality, sexual permissiveness, and
death.   At the same time dramatic series explored moral
issues in the shape of romantic anecdotes of the past, and
a daytime form, the soap opera, burst into prime time.
The Waltons and Little House on the Prairie promoted what

Earl Hammer, <u>Waltons</u>' creator, has called "pioneer virtues of thrift, industry, self-reliance, faith in God, trust in man, the Golden Rule."[7] Nighttime soaps, reigning champions of the ratings a few years later, presented the greed and folly of those who strayed from the Golden Rule: the rich and mighty of <u>Dallas</u>, <u>Knott's Landing</u>, and <u>Dynasty</u>. Concur- rently, two exceptional dramatic series, <u>Lou Grant</u> and <u>Hill Street Blues</u>, explored reality in instructive and entertaining ways.   Episodic television had evolved to new forms, and both the creators and the audience had become more sophis- ticated about the medium.

Those who work in the medium developed philosophi- cal, often opposing views of its output.   Network executive Bob Shanks asserted, "I believe America gets the television it wants, and largely needs, and the wonder to me is not how bad it is, but quite regularly, how extraordinarily good it is."[8] Writers Levinson and Link, who created <u>Mannix</u>, <u>McCloud</u>, and <u>Columbo</u>, demurred: "Risk is minimized as much as possible, and the reason television constantly imi- tates itself is the desperate hope that what worked before will work again....   Dealing with this instability [of the entertainment market], especially when millions of dollars are at stake, leads to a conservative way of doing busi- ness."[9]

Bob Shanks, the ABC executive quoted above, has since joined Fred Silverman, Lin Bolin, Bob Wood, and a legion of other network executives on the supply side of the business.   In a comparable switch, Grant Tinker, former head of MTM Enterprises, moved to the top position at NBC.   In such a move the perspective changes, perhaps changing the estimate of the medium's output as well.   What doesn't change and what both buyers and suppliers experience are the memos and meetings that define the process itself, the procedures of doing business.

DOING BUSINESS

Television shows are collaborative creations.   A writer or team of writers creates a script which is rewritten by the producers or staff writers.   Then the director and actors add their interpretations to the written words, as does the film or tape crew and the post-production staff.   Network representatives make comments and suggestions at several stages of the process, what some writers have called "back

seat driving."[10]   The aired version of the episode reflects
the opinion, fantasy, and vision of many--or of no one.

One of the by-products of the collaboration can be
the loss of what is bold and inventive.   The combined effort could create collective fantasy but more frequently the
process probably results in only what is safe and bland,
product more typical of committees than of creative genius.
Producer Alan Courtney declared, "The day of creative exchange between the networks and the creative community is
over.   It is mechanized, systematized ... and very, very
rarely what you see on the air turns out to be either the
concept, script or the casting that the creator had in mind
originally."[11]

Writers and producers must also contend with the
different visions or "creative differences" of contributors
other than network representatives.   Writer Patricia Jones
of the Bob Newhart Show, The Last Resort, and recently
Report to Murphy explained, "Producing a show is constant
negotiation in about forty different directions....   Everybody's seeing a narrow part of it.   What happens is that a
lot of the material gets compromised."   Her partner Donald
Reiker concurred, "The actor says, 'I'm breathing life into
these words,' and the writer is convinced that anybody could
do this if [he or she] would just say the lines.   And the set
director thinks his vision is what's important."[12]

Levinson and Link expressed similar sentiments about
creative differences on Columbo.   They wanted the series to
have a bright feeling but their camerman, Russ Metty, took
issue with that: "It's a cop show," he muttered to them.
"You want it to look like a goddamn musical?"[13]

Other factors affecting the output are the constraints
of time and the medium's capacious demand for product.
The system has an incessant requirement for new material,
which creates a constant burden for those who originate concepts and characters to produce quickly and continually.   Expectations for a staff writer-producer of episodic television
are to initiate, develop, and supervise twenty-two or more
plays a season, more than Ibsen's and Wilde's combined
lifetime output.   If the weekly fare isn't worthy of Ibsen or
Wilde it is partly because operating conditions work against
it.

The conditions of constantly creating under a deadline

require talents of their own: actors who are flexible and "quick studies," directors who can adapt new material quickly, and producers who can juggle multiple roles. During the season that a show is on the air the producers must cast future shows, monitor the results of the previous day's work, oversee the director, and debate their choices with network representatives. If they are writer-producers they are simultaneously preparing scripts for shooting, planning future scripts, and rewriting the script currently being rehearsed. The exacting schedule leaves little time for anything else, a circumstance wryly alluded to by the writer who said, "I like producing but I miss the sex."

The pace is seen as both a burden and a boon to those who work in television. Director Ida Lupino said, "Believe me, Bring it in on time is such a major factor in television that I'd sometimes get absolutely sick to my stomach days beforehand...."[14]

Yet the stress is exhilarating to others. Donald Reiker asserted, "There's instant gratification. I love the pressure. What a high it is. It's an impetus." Patricia Jones agreed, "It's demanding but there's a lot of action."[15]

More restrictive than even the demands of quantity and time, however, are the demands of taste. As a public medium, television reaches an audience of millions and its self-imposed task not to offend any of them is an effort of enormous proportion. The effort to be objectionable to no one, probably more than any other factor contributes to the homogenized, standardized program content which promotes replication from one television season to the next.

The writers and producers sometimes censor themselves purposefully or indirectly in the initial stages of presenting an idea. After all, the buyers, up until quite recently when cable programmers entered the market, were limited to three networks. "There are only three theatres for television," Norman Lear said in 1975. "If they are interested in buying a cop show, then that is what you as a craftsman must do because that's what the buyer wants."[16]

In this market, the low-risk attraction of the predictable and the tried and true prevails, and that which is original in concept or content is fearfully avoided. Ironically, among the most popular of all programs were innovative shows including All in the Family, Gunsmoke, and

Roots, which were actively resisted by network programmers until positive audience reaction assured their acceptance. Other innovative programs maybe never aired at all.   Thus does television become the victim of the insecurity and caution of its caretakers.

        The climate of caution prevailed in prime time for its first twenty years.   Controversy was taboo and therefore, as Levinson and Link noted, significant segments of American life were omitted: "In the recent past blacks were transformed into whites, ethnic backgrounds were replaced by vague and inoffensive Mittel-European antecedents, homosexuals didn't exist except in the limp-wristed routines of stand-up comics, and men and women never talked about sexual activities, much less indulged in them."[17]

        Critics of television's unreality, banality, and misrepresentation, some armed with social science research, organized and complained.   By the early 1980's networks, studios, and production companies had heard protest from both ends of the political spectrum and from some, like mothers of pre-schoolers, who were probably in the middle. Political, social, and religious groups espousing morality or espousing reform, denouncing change or the status quo, made their positions known.

        What had seemed harmless became, with the benefit of hindsight and research, heavy with implication.   Like suspects in a whodunit, prime time's creators were suddenly cloaked in inauspicious importance.   They were charged with putting ideas in our heads, peopling our collective fantasy, and making media models for us to copy.

        No one resigned as a result of the criticism and complaint.   However, many who worked in television reevaluated the medium and its place in our society.   Network executives acknowledged concern and occasional misgivings about the kinds of content that were being broadcast.   Producer Norman Lear conceded, "I'm concerned for what it is we're delivering for whatever impact it may have."[18]

        Other television professionals also considered the potential effects.   M*A*S*H's Alan Alda worried, "The unspoken assumptions are what mold the audience."[19]   Jim Brooks and Allen Burns (co-creators of The Mary Tyler Moore Show and the writers on Maude, Alice, Lou Grant, and Love Boat) evaluated their work in the light of the "unspoken assumptions" it hid, accepting the responsibility of communicating to the nation. [20]

In spite of the responsibility of constantly, inadvertently doing what Jim Brooks called "social comment," [21] and in spite of the pressure of coping with creative differences and working under deadline, most television people work in the industry because they enjoy it. Some, like the acclaimed film and television writer Fay Kanin, are motivated by the need to create, to express something "in your own terms." [22] Some are motivated by the financial rewards television offers its chosen people. Some want fame or what a comedy writer called "adulation and a good time." [23] Whatever their motives, their job satisfaction is high.

The words they use to describe their work reflect a childlike satisfaction. "I tell stories," Earl Hammer said simply. Others talked of "making people laugh," "fantasy," "creating make-believe." "It's fun being a boss," said producer Patricia Jones. "It's that feeling of wanting to express yourself. And get your own way." The words are something out of childhood. [24]

The work is something out of childhood, too: inventing people and stories, putting on a show. Levinson and Link work in Levinson's den debating for hours what imaginary people would do, what food they would eat, what clues they would leave at the scene of a crime. Comedy writing is even more like playing, consisting as it does of trading jokes and acting out comic routines. "We try things out beforehand," said Madelyn Davis. "Sure," her partner agreed, "sometimes I'd roll Madelyn up in a rug." [25]

In such a profession the work is its own reward. However, it is not its only reward. There is money to keep the wolf from the door, the awards from peers, and the applause of strangers. In addition there is the opportunity to create something original and marvelous, and show it to twenty, thirty, forty, or fifty million people, including former sweethearts and friends from the old neighborhood.

In spite of the constraints of time and taste and in spite of the medium's capacious demand for product of any quality, there have been and continue to be marvelously human characters and events portrayed on television screens. There are episodes of I Love Lucy, Mr. Peepers, The Odd Couple, and The Mary Tyler Moore Show that rank with the

best American comedy in any form.   Certain episodes of
The Defenders, The Waltons, Columbo, and Lou Grant can
compete with drama in any medium.

      But television's prime-time output represents sixty-
six hours of product a week, the bulk of which is neither
original nor marvelous.   Much of it the creators formed of
standard patterns of word and deed, of casts of common
character types.   Among the latter were the ladies who
were sirens and decoys and matriarchs and witches.   We
grew up with these creations.   Who they were and what
they said to us are examined in Part III.

PART III

★

THE THIRTY-YEAR IMAGE:
Female Character Types on
Episodic Television

One of the first and most enduring types of women heroes on prime-time television was a rambunctious rebel who was only intermittently heroic and seldom womanish. The character was a mischievous child-woman, the imp.

Like a tomboy she rejected the frills and fancies of her sex for the hardier advantages of the boys. Her figure and dress were boyish. She was active but awkward and graceless. In addition she was curious, imaginative, independent, adventuresome--and asexual. In all these things she resembled a pre-adolescent who wanted only to be a tomboy.

The imp wanted to have fun, to have adventures. She wanted to help humanity, rescue people, do good, and, if possible, become famous and wealthy, too. She was very like a male hero who was also typically active, adventuresome, athletic, imaginative, and independent.

However, for a female character, these attributes conflicted with society's expectations that she be a passive and dependent woman. Thus the imp, unlike the male hero, was restricted by the narrow boundaries of her sex role and, indeed, she did seem to be the antithesis of what psychologists described as the normal young woman: submissive, timid, dependent, domestic, emotional, sensitive, vain. With this definition of normal, the imp was in big trouble from the start and imp shows always dealt, to some extent at least, with the obvious conflict between her nature and behavior and society's expectations for her. This conflict was particularly evident in the most prominent television imp, Lucy Ricardo on the I Love Lucy Show.

21

Lucy was anything but passive, submissive, timid, and vain. On the contrary, she was rambunctious and rowdy. Like an awkward adolescent, she was so charged with energy that she frequently collided with the inanimate. Doors, walls, furniture became obstacles to the character's movement and she seemed to be in a constant conflict with her environment. Like other clown characters, Lucy's response to the conflict was exaggerated movement--bounding, sprawling, scrambling, recoiling--a jump where a skip would do.

The intensity of her activity and the force of her energies for her various projects and schemes and a range of expressions from outlandish pleasure to sepulchral gloom showed her dynamic qualities. Lucy was also active as a character, involved with the action of the drama and with the affairs of other characters. Although frequently admonished to "mind her own business" and "stay out of other people's lives," it was to Lucy's credit that she could not. She wanted to help, to know, to act. She wanted to be involved in the events of other people's lives--to assist Ricky's career, find a job for a foreign visitor, patch up a fight between her neighbors, the Mertzes.

Lucy was a pivotal character. Her actions initiated the actions and reactions of other characters. She was important to the development of the plot and frequently evolved the plot almost entirely through her own actions--buying a hat, auditioning for a singing role, or stopping the train by pulling a brake cord. What this female character said and did mattered--to the consequences of the plot, to the atmosphere of the show.

Lucy was an endearing character by being experimental and open to experience. She had no vanity and donned bizarre clothes and unbecoming postures, even impersonating a seal to accomplish a desired end. Her dedication to her schemes and dreams was epitomized in her zest and energy in attempting to execute them. The considerable comic talents of Lucille Ball, with her boundless energy and expressive face, undoubtedly contributed to the attractiveness of this imp, but even portrayed by another actor, the character's boisterous energy for ideas and plans and her uninhibited enthusiasm for her family and friends would have been appealing.

For all the appeal of the character, however, the role was not one which invited awe or emulation. The char-

The considerable comic talents of Lucille Ball, with her
boundless energy and expressive face, contributed to the attractiveness of this imp, yet she was not heroic but an imperfect being whose energy and action led to some disastrous
results.

acter was not heroic but an imperfect being whose energy and action led to some disastrous results. She had little power and few resources other than her own energy and artifice to deal with the confusion and disorder which followed in her wake.

The havoc she wreaked and the trouble she caused frequently arose from some conflict with an authority figure or other symbol of the established order. Seemingly without guile, she exaggerated the authority of any petty bureaucrat she encountered; she addressed a Bureau of Immigration agent as "your honor," a police officer as "Mr. Detective-Sir." Yet her natural inclination to satisfy her own needs and ignore rules invariably resulted in some problems with authority. In one episode it was Gale Gordon as the conductor warning her sternly, "We have rules, you know."[1] In another episode, Lucy's adversary was a self-satisfied television station owner who used his power and position to Lucy's eventual demise.

Even her husband represented an authority figure, cajoling and admonishing Lucy to follow the rules, let the police handle it, stay out of trouble. Lucy's response to her difficulties with Ricky and others was some devious and circuitous plan to achieve her denied goal. At these times she appeared particularly childish and irresponsible. In an effort to prevent Ricky from learning that he had been fired because of her, she tried (unsuccessfully) to pull, break, and bite the telephone cord in one memorable scene. In another episode she responded to a gunman who was threatening her, "I made a boo boo?"[2]

Consistent with her pattern of irresponsibility, she never acknowledged rule-breaking as wrong but placated the authority or power figure and continued to follow whatever action she'd set upon. In a typical episode, she "disobeyed" Ricky's instructions to ignore the man in the next train compartment, to keep quiet about her observations, and to keep out of police business. She pulled the train brake cord, three times stopping the train, after repeated protestations from the conductor, looking guilty and contrite when Ethel Mertz said accusingly, "Lucy! What happened?" In spite of her apparent contrition Lucy did not hesitate to transgress again.

Her transgressions most frequently occurred in the area of housewifery. There she showed that--except for her

economic dependence on her husband--she could in no way
fulfill society's expectations for her. She was incapable of
being a homemaker, too self-oriented to be a devoted wife.

Lucy's impulse to follow her own bent with single-
minded dedication led to scatterbrained distraction--forgetting
names, misplacing her purse, losing keys and tickets. And
it contributed to her incompetence in the performance of all
the skills and tasks related to her role as housewife--paying
bills, renewing insurance, keeping appointments, cooking,
decorating, making decisions, and toasting bread.

She was apparently incapable in related adult roles as
well. Although sexual life was a taboo subject for fifties'
television, from what we know about Lucy it wouldn't seem
to be her strong suit either. To her husband there was little demonstration of affection or sexual validation. In episodes in which she tried to attract another man's attention,
she was a failure as a femme fatale (resorting instead to a
childish ruse--feigned sickness--in one episode).

Her capabilities as a mother we could only guess
since she was never shown bathing, dressing, changing, or
feeding her child. Nor did she cart around the bottles,
diapers, and other paraphernalia that real mothers carry
when they travel or visit with a baby. In several episodes
her own mother was the caretaker of her child, leaving
Lucy free to engage in scatterbrained schemes and trouble-
making.

Not only Lucy but Ethel, too, was extraordinarily incompetent, having few domestic skills or little ability to perform routine activities, such as driving a car or keeping an
appointment. Ethel's and Lucy's incompetence in domestic
tasks may have been a sort of silent rebellion against the
role for which they were so obviously unsuited. The impression of silent rebellion was strengthened by their evident attraction to more glamorous and rewarding roles. It was
their particular misfortune that they were bound to fail in
these roles, too.

The economic dependence of these two characters encouraged elaborate get-rich-quick schemes and business ventures which usually resulted in economic disaster. In a
graphic episode filmed in 1954, Lucy and Ethel decided to
bottle and market Lucy's homemade salad dressing. Without the resources to market such a product in large quanti-

ties, it would have been an extensive undertaking in any case, but their failure to evaluate their costs and to price the product at a profit doomed the venture, as Ricky had predicted.

However, most of the conflict with Ricky occurred not because of ventures in the marketplace, but because of Lucy's mostly ineffectual schemes to break into show business. In various episodes she costumed and corsetted herself, cajoled directors, and impersonated musicians and patrons for a chance to be chosen for stage or screen.

The entertainment world seemed to be an important symbol in the Lucy plots and Ricky's position in it was a source of jealousy and wistfulness for Lucy. For Ricky it was an occupation, a career in which he sought success and acclaim. For Lucy its attraction was more complex. It represented a glamorous world to Lucy, and she was often jealous of the singers, actresses, and other female entertainers Ricky encountered in his work.

Show business represented more than glamour to Lucy, however. Film critic Molly Haskell has argued persuasively that its appeal may be not only romantic but also practical. It is a vehicle for prestige and power, whereby a woman could succeed without being aggressive and masculine. By utilizing natural "female" talents of play-acting, mimicking, dancing, and singing, Lucy Ricardo reasoned (in nine of the first season's scripts), she could achieve fame and fortune. Ethel, too, shared Lucy's stagestruck desires, but pursued her dreams less vigorously.

Essential to the definition of the imp character at this time was the trait of incompetence. Lucy was inept as a housewife and equally incapable of success in the marketplace or above the footlights. Furthermore, her ineptitude had disastrous results. Her thoughtless actions in the pursuit of whatever she momentarily wanted threatened (with alarming regularity) the economic security of the family or the emotional stability of a marriage, her own or someone else's. Her distraction led to destruction and her incompetence was the cause of chaos, disorder, and confusion.

It can be argued that the image of incompetence and distraction was necessary to the comedy of the character. Gracie Allen, Joan Davis, Imogene Coca, and other female comics portrayed imps, and male actors of the period (Ozzie

Nelson, Jackie Gleason, William Bendix) portrayed inept
oafs who frequently found themselves in untenable positions
from which they needed rescue by their wives or children.
Since male and female comics alike portrayed inept characters, we might conclude that a certain comic type requires
incompetence and ineptitude.

The difference between male and female incompetents,
however, is a matter of perspective. The male incompetents were frequently "balanced" with at least one male character demonstrating capability. David Nelson, Ozzie's oldest
son on the Ozzie and Harriet episodes, was an example.
And, in any event, the dominant images on television were
of competent males, so a few comic figures did not make
the norm. However, the imps of the period (nine introduced
between 1949 and 1954 alone) were invariably incompetent,
with few models to serve as exceptions. Certainly the I Love
Lucy Show offered no exceptional, capable female "opposites"
for the incompetent Lucy and Ethel characters, although such
foils are a common comic device.

By the 1960's the imp was single. Freed from the
domestic scene, she was no longer an inept housewife. She
had newfound competence--in wrestling, riding horseback,
racing cars. Her competence did not extend to traditionally
female pursuits, however, and she was as much a rebel
against the social definition of appropriately female as her
predecessors had been.

The most delightful imps of the decade appeared in
rustic clothing. In Western settings there were television's
renditions of frontierswomen Ann Oakley and Jane Canarray
in stories which showed how their presence disturbed and
disordered the community. And in comedy there was the
displaced country bumpkin Elly Mae Clampett of Beverly
Hillbillies, who was part of a whole clan whose presence
disturbed the community.

⌈ The humor of the popular Beverly Hillbillies was
based on a family of characters who defied conventions and
expectation; Elly Mae was no exception. She could not sub-
ordinate her irrepressible spirit and would not submit to
domination or admit that she was less than any man.⌉ She
was in constant revolt against the restrictions imposed by
an alien society--contemporary urban society. When she
wanted to join the marines, her father observed "It says
here they can build men but I don't see how they can build
one outta you. "[3]

The humor of the popular <u>Beverly Hillbillies</u> was based on a family of characters who <u>defied conventions</u> and expectations. Diane Douglas's imp character Elly Mae (standing) was no exception.

Being independent, adventurous, and athletic, she
swam with the dolphins at an amusement park and out-
wrestled a wrestling champion. Disarmingly direct, she
threw a would-be beau over her shoulder for bending to
kiss her hand because, as she explained, "he was fixing to
bite me."[4] She could not act as if she were an ornament
for men's pleasure.

Nor would she dress the part. She was too curvy
to look boyish, but her jeans, moccasins, and men's hats
somewhat masked her female shape. When she did dress
in the latest feminine fashions, as she did in one episode,
she didn't go as far as to don the crippling footgear of the
season and so appeared as the Beverly Hills fashionplate
only down to her (bare) feet.

Another buckskin lass appeared on a 1968 episode of
Bonanza, the popular Western about rancher Ben Cartwright
and his three sons. The episode evolved around the relationship of son Little Joe and a new-found friend, "Cal," a
short form of Calamity Jane. Cal's presentation of herself
early in the episode is best described by saying she was
mistaken for a boy by the other male Cartwrights. However, a bath and a dress transformed her into a conventional-
looking female, and led to her toying with the idea of becoming a "lady." The way she defined it, a "lady" was a
married woman who wore dresses and went to dances.

Cal's own life was less ceremonial and as the story
developed it became evident that she had saved Little Joe's
life in an Indian raid and that she could shoot, ride horses,
and swim with skill and agility. She was also friendly with
outlaws and afraid of no one. An excerpt of an exchange
with the legendary Doc Holliday portrayed her spirit and
independence:

> Doc: You're going away with me now.
>
> Cal: I ain't going nowhere with you--let alone
> marrying you.
>
> Doc: And (what about) him?
>
> Cal: I don't know. He might be just the thing for
> me to settle down with. And be a lady.
>
> Doc: A lady! You will never be a lady.... And
> I'll kill the man who tries to take you from
> me. ...

> <u>Cal:</u>   If you harm Lil' Joe, I'm gonna' blow your
>   head off. [5]

The contrast between Cal's tough stance with Holliday,
a known killer, and her talk of becoming a lady was height-
ened by the vision of her sitting at the bar in silk creations
while drinking whiskey.   In addition to her drinking habits
were her spontaneous, exaggerated gestures and colorful
speech--"Keep your pants on ... ain't you never seen a
lady before?   ... I never could cotton to a fellow who
couldn't hold his liquor."

The image Cal portrayed was heroic. She was
courageous and competent. She was inventive, as shown
by her devising a means to keep Holliday from killing Joe
in the dance hall scene.   Physically, she was portrayed
very differently from the buxom Calamity Jane in history
books; her flat-chested, athletic figure like that of an adolescent male was reminiscent of a "tomboy."

There were few true imps of the 1960s.   What we
saw instead were a host of superhuman females with extraordinary powers which they subordinated to please their
husband-masters.   Their subtle rebellion against the restriction of normal domestic life was portrayed by the covert use of their awesome powers, action which invariably
threatened the tranquillity and economic security of their
mates.   In their rebellion and their nuisance effect they
resembled the imps of the fifties.   They were not simply
imp characters, however, but a distinct sixties television
phenomenon, and as such they are more fully discussed in
Chapter 11:   The Witch.

In the seventies, television imps were represented
by the athletic Sabrina of <u>Charlie's Angels,</u> a character like
Cal who could ride horses and shoot guns, and by the mentally keen, mechanically able Irene Lorenzo of <u>All in the
Family</u>.   Another comic imp of the decade was Penny Marshall's character Laverne De Fazio of <u>Laverne and Shirley,</u>
the continuing story of two working-class women who struggled without education or obvious talent to better themselves.

The rebellious, rowdy Laverne duplicated the imp
character made popular by Lucille Ball twenty years before.
Like Ball's imp she was dynamic and destructive, falling
over furniture and knocking other characters into water or
out of windows.   The disastrous effects of her actions

The rebellious, rowdy Laverne of <u>Laverne and Shirley</u> duplicated the imp character made popular by Lucille Ball twenty
years before.

dramatized that her energies and ideas were out of harmony
with the rest of the world and with what the world expected
her to be. In one episode she mastered a forty-second ob-
stacle course only to have Shirley innocently remark, "Any
girl who can run that course in forty seconds is nothing but
a freak."[6]

Laverne was not exactly a freak, but an inappropriate
female. She was too bold and tough to act like the "weaker"
sex. Her actions, which would have been acceptable in an
adolescent boy, were the source of humor:

> Laverne: I broke my tooth.
>
> Shirley: How many times have I told you not to go
> around opening beer bottles with your
> teeth?[7]
>
> . . .
>
> Hughes: You probably think all women should be
> soft and sweet and feminine. No one can
> say that about these women.
>
> Laverne: Yeah! (Mixed reaction.)[8]

The inappropriateness of the imp's actions was under-
lined by the absence of romantic attention from men. Neither Lucy nor the unmarried Laverne had a romantic, emotionally satisfying relationship, yet other types of characters
did. Lucy was highly involved with husband Ricky, but it
was a relationship characterized more by his paternal control and her manipulation and deceit than by expressions of
intimacy, trust, and spontaneous affection. One wondered
why Lucy and Ricky stayed married unless duplicity and
dueling provided satisfaction. There were men in Laverne's
life, but they were friends not lovers. Thus, neither Lucy
nor Laverne was provided with a completely satisfying male-
female relationship.

Both Ball and Marshall were conventionally attractive,
an impression maybe modified by the characters' tendencies
to grimace and gape and collide with inanimate objects. And
their commitment to friends and passion for their projects
were surely attractive qualities. Yet their energetic passion
and physical attractiveness were somehow not sexy. They
didn't translate as traits which appealed to men. There was
some flaw manifest in their actions or personalities which
prevented them from being sexually attractive.

Perhaps the flaw was their inability to conform, to play the selfless, feminine game.   Perhaps it was that both sought selfhood on their own terms, rejecting a role which offered a hardworking, basically uneventful life of passivity and dependence and devotion to others.   Or else we must conclude that dynamic, imaginative, passionate female characters are not sexually attractive!

If the imp was inept and irresponsible as a homemaker, the goodwife was her opposite. She was Miss Domestic, a paragon in the home. Besides being competent at dishes and dusting, she was attractive, good-natured, and wise--a jewel in any family crown.

The goodwife's only interest was family and house, the focus of all meaningful action. The complementary arenas of the home and the outside world were assigned as feminine and masculine spheres, according to the typical scenario. While males conquered dragons in government and industry, females vanquished dustballs in playrooms and closets. The goodwife liked this arrangement.

Her setting was the home and she was seldom seen outside it. Her uniform was the apron and, later, the housedress. Her sphere of influence was limited to domestic concerns, but within the home the goodwife exercised considerable personal power, making decisions, advising, and chastising family members. In interpersonal relationships among family members, her contribution was wise counsel and moral guidance.

In spite of obvious competence and capability within the home setting, the goodwife had no compunction to test her mettle outside the home arena. She was pictured as content with her household and family duties, however unglamorous the actual chores may have been. Her identification was with the family and there her satisfaction lay, as well.

Typical goodwife characters appeared in situation

34

comedies throughout the fifties: The Aldrich Family, Make Room for Daddy, Father Knows Best, The Stu Erwin Show, Life with Father, Pride of the Family, and The Life of Riley, among other shows, depicted this character type. Dramatic shows that featured the goodwife include Dragnet, Big Town, and Gunsmoke. Harriet Nelson of The Adventures of Ozzie and Harriet presented a classic example of goodwife.

The Adventures of Ozzie and Harriet was a comedy which originated in 1952 and aired until 1966. It concerned the activities of the Nelson family--Ozzie, Harriet, and their two sons, David and Ricky. The adventures, however, were primarily Ozzie's; Harriet had no adventures of her own, but contributed to nearly every scene lines like, "Oh, that's a good idea" and "It's okay with me, dear."

Harriet's homemaking activities were evident in near-ly every episode: caring for family members, preparing food, serving dinner, dusting walls and furniture. In most of these scenes she wore an apron; in one episode, she ap-peared with her hair in curlers in the scenes in which she was not aproned. Hers was not a glamorous role.

The goodwife's image, though banal, was one of a competent female. In contrast to the scatterbrained, idiot-wife presented on series I Love Lucy, I Married Joan, and Burns and Allen, she was an efficient household manager, skillfully executing domestic tasks and managing household affairs. Like the shows The Life of Riley, The Honey-mooners, and The Trouble with Father, the main female character of Ozzie and Harriet may have appeared compe-tent in juxtaposition to the image of the primary male char-acter, a bumbling, inept husband-father. Unlike Ozzie who misplaced keys, mistook people, and misread intentions, and who bumped into walls, slipped on rugs, and tangled himself in firehoses, Harriet performed competently and offered a calm voice of reason in more than one crisis.

To interpersonal confrontations, Harriet responded calmly as well. She was good-natured and accepting of her husband's foibles and idiosyncrasies. In an episode entitled "Volunteer Fireman," she let Ozzie carry her upstairs like a sack of laundry on his back to give him practice in res-cues. To his unreasonable demands that she limit her phone calls to thirty seconds and his incessant interruptions during her phone conversation, Harriet responded with even-tempered tolerance. In other episodes, she promoted a

course of restraint and common sense in dealing with their sons, friends, and neighbors.

Capable in personal confrontations as well as household activities, Harriet was nevertheless confined as a character to family and household concerns. She was seldom depicted in tasks other than domestic chores and her recreation, too, was centered on the home. When Ozzie identified typical activities of each family member in one episode, Harriet was described as "reading a magazine" in the living room. She apparently had no outside interests other than the care and concerns of her family, and even her phone conversations involved descriptions of what Ozzie or their sons were doing.

In general, women on the show were involved in provincial pursuits. They were depicted as creatures who cried easily, who were concerned with personal appearance, and who nagged male characters about wearing ties, brushing their hair, being on time. In one episode David worried that his girlfriend would be angry if he were late to dinner. "Do you want Susan to be mad at me?" he complained to Ricky. "Boy, hen-pecked already,"[1] Ricky reacted. A similar commentary on women occurred in the fireman episode:

> Harriet: You know, if they let women join the fire department then I'd see more of you.
>
> Ozzie: Are you kidding? You gals take too long to dress.
>
> Harriet: Oh, I don't know--we can be pretty quick.
>
> Ozzie: By the time you got your make-up on, the fire'd be out.[2]

Harriet's identification with family members as the source of her character definition was so complete that she did not contemplate joining the fire force to do community good, as Ozzie and neighbor Thorny had, but simply to be near her husband. She was a secondary, somewhat passive character, whose actions were limited to reacting to the behavior of others, rather than initiating any action herself.

[Opposite:] In The Adventures of Ozzie and Harriet, the adventures were primarily Ozzie's; Harriet had no adventures of her own.

This secondary stature was not unique to the character of Harriet Nelson but was typical of other goodwife characters of most popular comedies.   They were not so evident
on dramatic programs, where the action was seldom set in
the home.   Occasionally the domestic goodwife character appeared in a small role on a dramatic show, portraying a female adjunct to a dominant, active male character.

An early Dragnet, for example, depicted just such a
character in the image of Fay Smith, the wife of officer
Frank Smith.   She tended to the comforts of the male characters, serving them, helping with their coats, asking after
them.   Her particular concern was her husband and his hap-
piness.   Frank indicated this was so in an explanation about
some expensive camera equipment he'd acquired: "Fay gave
it to me--saved the money out of her allowance."[3]

Fay's secondary status in relation to her husband was
more pronounced than Harriet Nelson's and she was less developed as a character.   She had none of the wit and force
of the Nelson character.   However, she was in other ways
a copy of the comedy version of the stereotype.   She was
competent, tolerant, and sacrificing.   Her actions involved
caring for the house and catering to the needs of other
household members.   She was so selfless that she used her
"allowance" for a gift for her husband.

The image of women as selfless, supportive, and
sympathetic bystanders to male heroics was so central to
the concept of female characters by the late 1950's that it
carried over to dramatic programming in which the apron
and the dust rag were seldom to be seen.   Dedicated sup-
porters of the male characters' interests and activities,
female characters of many dramas of the period acted like
heroes' wives.   Devoted, competent, attractive, good-
natured, and wise, these women were goodwives but for the
setting.   Thus, in the public settings of courtroom, office,
and hospital was a sort of office goodwife and in the Western setting we saw the boardinghouse or store goodwife,
examples of a type which might be called the professional
goodwife.

The professional goodwife was, like the domestic
version, a secondary character, dependent for her actions
on the plans and movements of the hero.   She was passive
--both submissive and inactive.   Her function in her relationship with the hero was to be appreciative, concerned,

Professional goodwife dedicated her life to the hero's work, participating vicariously in his victories in the hospital, the courthouse, the world. Elena Verdugo in the role of Consuelo Lopez of <u>Marcus Welby, M.D.</u> portrayed a goodwife and one of the rare minority women in an on-going prime time role. Here she is flanked by Robert Young (left) and James Brolin.

and helpful when required, sacrificing her own desires and interests if necessary.

She was notably inactive, serving primarily as a sounding board for the hero's musings and deliberations. She did not ride the range with the Western hero or chase criminals with the lawyer or private eye, as a male associate would have done. Instead, she listened to the hero's ideas and ideals, applauded his exploits, and consoled him in his moments of self doubt and defeat.

A fine example of the professional goodwife character was seen in a popular program of the 1950's called Big Town. The newspaper format of this show featured Steve Wilson, the managing editor of a New York newspaper, and Diane Walker, his girlfriend. Walker, supposedly a commercial artist, was never portrayed at her work. She carried no sketch pad, drew no sketches, and had no deadlines. She was seen as goodwife, however.

Diane Walker was alternately consoling or enouraging Steve Wilson throughout their encounters--making him coffee, extolling his work. She was concerned that he was taking too many risks. She was understanding and supportive when his work separated them.

She was also passive. Wilson's interests and Wilson's articles were the topics of their conversations, even though she must have had creative activities of her own. The ardor and enterprise of the creative person, too, were missing in her scenes with him, as she performed no actions on her own initiative, but only if Wilson asked it of her. Like a passive receptacle, she absorbed his offerings, even carried messages to him and from him. The line, "Miss Walker, can you get a message to Mr. Wilson?" was repeated in several episodes. Her willingness to relay messages, along with other of her characteristics, was evident in the restaurant conversation excerpted below:

Steve: Darling, I don't have very much time.

Diane: Oh, and I had such plans....

Steve: I won't have time to eat. You go ahead and order....

Diane: Anything I can do?

Steve: Maybe. You know R. C. Hall, don't you?

Diane: Know him? I've been in his presence. He
         smiled at me.

Steve: He's honorary chairman of your heart fund,
         isn't he? Maybe you can arrange a meeting
         for me. You're a resourceful woman.

Diane: Well, I'll try.

Steve: You may have to. I have to go now.

Diane: I'll be around. [4]

Walker's willing accommodation to Steve's needs was
not unattractive. On the contrary, her understanding of and
tolerance for the demands of Wilson's work were positive
and supportive. Her own needs for emotional support and
reinforcement were never addressed, however. Her sacrifice and devotion were evident, yet Wilson's sacrifices for
her career commitments were never shown.

The prevalence of the professional goodwife type is
suggested by the number and variations of this character
which appeared on television screens of the late fifties:
Perry Mason's glamorous Della Street; Cimarron City's
boardinghouse keeper Beth Purcell; storekeepers Milly Scott
(Rifleman) and Laura Thomas (Johnny Ringo); the discreet
"Sam" of Richard Diamond; and the beautiful Suzanne Fabray
on 77 Sunset Strip.

The appeal of these characters may have been for the
unthreatening way by which they combined gainful employment
and an emotionally supportive relationship with the male heroes. Although the professional goodwife worked outside the
home, her work demanded little commitment or effort on her
part and no concessions from the male hero. Thus, she repeatedly demonstrated for male viewers that a career woman
could be a devoted and undemanding associate, as reliably
supportive as the domestic goodwife. Moreover, since she
worked in the same arena as the male hero, she was frequently on hand to encourage his adventures and exploits or
commiserate in his defeats. Her own occupation in service
work or clerical work (never the dramatic hero's fields),
coupled with her lower status eliminated the threat of her
usurping his place in the work world. She was not competitive with him since she was never in the same game but
was rather the cheerleader to his ballplaying.

For female viewers she was reassuring, as well, for

she demonstrated that a woman could succeed at having a job without endangering her credentials as a female.   As boardinghouse keeper, storekeeper, hotelkeeper, or nurse, the goodwife performed maternal tasks for a surrogate family: serving food, making beds, ministering to the needs of others.   As private secretary, receptionist, or switchboard operator, the goodwife worked for a surrogate husband, an impression enhanced by her presentation as unmarried and committed to her job; like a devoted wife, she dedicated her life to his work, participating vicariously in his victories in the courtroom, in the marketplace, in the world.   The goodwife's work therefore represented an extension of her female nature and not an aggressive pursuit of prestige and power. Often her success in retaining her "feminine" appeal was attested to by the male hero's romantic interest.

The popularity of the professional goodwife type beginning in the late fifties and continuing through the midseventies, the same historic period in which more American females attained gainful employment than ever before, quite likely represented a response to that surge of women into the workforce and the resulting anxieties that it created for both sexes.   The life of professional goodwife was a safe, albeit indistinguished and uneventful, alternative to the domestic one idealized on situation comedies of every primetime season of the period.

The domestic goodwife continued to thrive throughout the 1960's and scores of examples of the type were introduced to prime time in the first half of the decade.   The sixties' version of the domestic type was even more pronounced in situation comedies than it had been the decade before, when it was eclipsed by active, pivotal imp characters like Gracie Allen, Liz Cooper, Joan Stevens, and the irrepressible Lucy Ricardo.   By the 1960 season, the imp shows had disappeared from the top twenty and, except for the goodwife, women had vanished as well.   Of the ten top-rated shows of the season, only Gunsmoke and Real McCoys featured women among their regular characters (and by 1962 the McCoys' entrant had "died").   Womanless casts peopled the frontier and rural settings and single father households proliferated the popular programs of the early sixties.   The exceptions were seen in typical contemporary settings, prominent among which was The Dick Van Dyke Show.

In the person of Mary Tyler Moore, The Dick Van

In contrast to Harriet Nelson's somewhat wry view of her role and the imp's positive distaste for it, Laura Petrie (Mary Tyler Moore), presenting a picture of America's childhood sweetheart grown up, wholeheartedly endorsed the goodwife role in The Dick Van Dyke Show.

Dyke Show presented Laura Petrie, the most perfect of
domestic goodwife characters.   Laura, married to television
writer Rob Petrie, depicted a wife and mother who was attractive, competent, kind, considerate, and conscientious.
The goodwife image portrayed by this character was more
idealistic than that of the popular 1950's programs; hers was
a privileged life, almost glamorous.

Laura was a contented character; she was a former
dancer whose role as homemaker was still attractive and
satisfying to her.   Her household activities included giving
large dinner parties and having friends over for coffee and
cake.   She was appreciated and applauded by her husband
who greeted her warmly each evening, bragged about her,
and brought her presents:

> Rob: Hi.   Take off your apron--an empress doesn't
>   wear an apron....
>
> Laura: I'm sorry, Your Majesty.   It's just that I've
>   been scrubbing the palace floors all day and
>   doing the king's laundry....   [fingering Rob's
>   gift],   What's the occasion?
>
> Rob: No occasion....   It's just your job to wear
>   it and enjoy it. [5]

Although she had jobs more tedious than wearing
Rob's presents--chores and errands that were part of the
housewife's lot--being honored by her husband and valued
by her friends and neighbors was clearly part of the image,
too.   In contrast to Harriet Nelson's somewhat wry view of
her role and the imp's positive distaste for it, Laura Petrie, presenting a picture of America's childhood sweetheart
grown up, wholeheartedly endorsed the goodwife role.

Her opposite was represented by the character Sally
Rogers, the comedy writer in Rob's work family.   Cynical
(whereas Laura was trusting) and a wise-cracking comic,
she contrasted with the sweet and gentle goodwife:

> Buddy: I got a feeling this kid's the worst comedian
>   since the beginning of time.
>
> Sally: You forget I saw you perform. [6]

The privileged status of the goodwife's lot in life was
highlighted by the spinster Rogers, whose discontent distinguished her.   Ostensibly Sally Rogers was a success symbol

--a career woman with a glamorous, well-paying job. She
was conventionally attractive, competent in her work. Laura,
who had been in show business before marriage and still appreciated the footlights, might have felt jealous of Rogers.
But it was evident that Sally herself was dissatisfied and in-
secure. Her life was emotionally unfulfilling, despite her
accomplishments and competencies, because she didn't have
a man in it. She and Laura together represented the Before
and After of an American stereotype: career woman in
search of marriage so as to be fulfilled. Sally, single and
man-desperate, represented Before, and Laura, contentedly
married, portrayed the ideal After.

        Laura Petrie was not unique as the idealized good-
wife. Other examples of the type were seen in The Danny
Thomas Show, Leave It to Beaver, and The Donna Reed
Show. Besides their urban, middle-class, WASP back-
grounds, the series, including Van Dyke, have in common
the idealization of the goodwife as the embodiment of all
that is socially and ethically correct and also the endorsement of homemaking as the one true path for women. The
first condition presented the goodwife as the ideal, a paragon of social and moral behavior. The second presented
her role as the ideal female role.

        The goodwife as paragon portrayed the character as
the personification of wisdom and virtue whose presence en-
abled and refined the male hero. Although tolerant and
sensitive toward others, Laura and the other goodwife characters were nevertheless capable of advising and admonishing male characters to do the correct and ethical thing.
Even physically, Laura and other female characters were
upright and correct, their posture straight and square-
shouldered. They contrasted with the male characters, who
lounged on arm chairs and leaned against walls. In discussions the males were depicted as stubborn, almost amoral,
unsocialized beings, guided by the gentle dictates of their
wives.

        The importance of the goodwife's function as moral
and social guide was evident in the frequent episodes in
which husband or children were tempted to act in a manner
which was irresponsible, immoral, or uncouth. Through
the goodwife's advice or silent example, their erring ways
were corrected, and order and decency were restored once
again. Goodwife's contribution was underscored by the single father shows Bachelor Father, My Three Sons, The Andy

Griffith Show, and Family Affair in which personal and family
matters were resolved only with great effort.

The potential for chaos and trouble inherent to the
single-father households, the obvious contentment and good
fortune of the goodwife, and the dissatisfaction of a character like Sally Rogers together argued the rightness of the
goodwife role. The single-father format demonstrated the
difficulties a family encounters without a goodwife and the
unhappy careergirl character demonstrated the difficulties a
woman encounters without a man, her only recourse to marriage being the surrogate wifedom of the professional goodwife. Thus, the goodwife's life was shown to be the best of
all possible female lives.

By the seventies prime-time programming was providing a greater variety of realistic female characters than
had previous decades, including middle-aged Maude, news-
woman Mary Richards, and the divorced mother of One Day
at a Time, Ann Romano. However, the primary setting for
females on top-rated shows of the period was still domestic
with regular characters as goodwives, such as All in the
Family, The Jeffersons, The Waltons, Good Times, Happy
Days, and Little House on the Prairie. Except for the
shows set in the romantic past (Waltons and Little House),
the change seemed to be that the goodwife's lot was more
laden with duties than privileges. Like the long-suffering
wife on The Honeymooners, the seventies' image was of a
housewife burdened with duties and chores, whose deference
and secondary status to her husband was highly visible. The
domestic figure of Edith Bunker on All in the Family provided the decade's representative example.

A Queens, New York, housewife, Edith was primarily
concerned with her family--husband Archie, daughter Gloria,
and son-in-law Michael Stivic--and with family members'
various problems encountered within and outside the home.
She herself rarely left the home except to grocery shop or
go to church. Her life offered few diversions other than
television and the conversation of friends, and her home offered little comfort for the enjoyment of either.

The goodwife role enacted by Edith Bunker had none
of the glamour and little of the satisfaction evident in the
story of the sixties' goodwife. Fulfilling the family's expectations that she clean the house and prepare and serve
food, Edith's rewards typically were complaints and insults.

<u>All in the Family</u> appealed to females as well as male view-
ers, especially the characters of Edith (center) and Gloria.
Like Archie, Edith expressed nostalgia for the "old days"
and served to reassure family-centered women that the old
values were still important.

In addition, the home, the domain of the sixties goodwife,
was usurped at will by her husband.   In an episode in which
he feigned a back injury, Archie complained that he was reduced to using Edith's chair.   In another episode when Edith
said she was having a private phone conversation, he responded, "Private?   This is my house, my living room, and
that's my phone.   I am in on all the privates in this house."[7]

Edith's secondary status was suggested in her demeanor, as well as by the absence of territorial rights.   In
one episode she and Archie had a conflict over Gloria, yet
she never physically confronted Archie, but leaned her body
toward him, one shoulder pulled back, as if ready to dodge
a blow.   When pursuing Archie with a point, she followed
immediately behind, with a mincing shuffle, resembling a
child on tiptoes.   Too, her conciliatory pleas and high-
pitched voice were suggestive of a child asking favors from
an adult.

Yet in spite of her inferior stature in the household,
she represented the woman of virtue whose goodness and
prudence would guide the family.   Selfless and unselfcon-
scious, Edith was less moralistic than her predecessors.
Rarely would she deliberately provoke disagreement, although she could be forceful in the pursuit of some greater
good as she demonstrated in occasional confrontations with
Archie.

She was Archie's moral opposite, open and accepting
of others, her tolerance in obvious contrast to Archie's big-
otry.   Another evident contrast was between Edith's honesty
and Archie's dissembling duplicity.   Innocently she uncovered
the hypocrisy of his moral posing.   At other times she
served as the foil for his shady deals and questionable
schemes.

Her own actions served as the moral barometer by
which the audience might gauge the propriety and morality
of the other characters' behaviors.   She was not patroniz-
ing, however, but unconsciously and spontaneously good.
Her virtue was its own lesson.

Her virtue was also its own reward.   Although she
was a sensitive person, she was protected from personal
hurt by her own naivete and the optimistic belief that people were basically good.   Incapable of noting sarcasm or
subterfuge, she took things at their face value.   Her inex-

perience and innocence limited Edith's understanding of
events and people, yet her literal-mindedness did not prevent her from grasping emotional truths.   Archie's insults
were unheard, and she responded instead to his unspoken
need for her.

The long-suffering goodwife as portrayed by Edith
(and Louise Jefferson and Florida Evans) was not unsympathetic.   Her dedication to and support for family members
and friends was appealingly selfless.   However, it led to
Edith's total dependence on Archie and Gloria for her hap-
piness, even for stimulation.   As the series developed this
changed somewhat as Edith's occasional demonstrations of
assertion made the character healthier, less dependent, and
more interesting.

The goodwife, worrying about Archie or Rob or Bud or Ricky, was the picture of selfless absorption, attention which was taken for granted by husband, children, neighbors, and friends. Her polar opposite was the harpy: an aggressive, single woman, more predator than preyed upon, and never taken for granted. The harpy was strong, even overpowering, and she marshalled force and energy in pursuit of her objective, the capture of the man of her affections.

A classic example of the hunt was performed by Jane Hathaway in pursuit of young Jethro Bodine of Beverly Hillbillies. Bodine, childlike and giant-sized, was an overgrown farm boy. His slow wit was no match for the wiles of Hathaway, but his innocence seemed to shield him from her grasp. In an episode in which he was to enlist in the military service, she brought him a "pin-up picture" of herself on a bear rug--a gesture which he accepted with naive good cheer. Another Hathaway ploy was her spy test whereby she persuaded Bodine to try his skill as spy-catcher by coaxing her with kisses. His cautious enticement caused her to offer encouraging words even as she played hard-to-get.

The harpy's seduction scenes were always incongruous combinations of actions both bold and coy. She went to great trouble to appear nonchalant; she moved mountains and then acted passive and vapid. Her invitation was too obvious, and the power of her personality was too thinly disguised beneath a veneer of fragility and submission.

The contradictions inherent to the character were the source of the humor. She was a career woman, competent

50

and financially independent, yet committed to dependence and compliance with men. Her actions were ludicrous, over-blown, exaggerated. She was greedy for life, rapacious in her quest for love, yet feminine, precise, and pristine.

Sue Ann Nivens of The Mary Tyler Moore Show exemplified the contrasts the harpy presented. Nivens' career as television chef combined domesticity and the bright lights in an uneasy union. It was accentuated by her aggressive pursuit of power off-camera and her on-camera persona as sugar and spice. Her dress and decor, all hearts and lace, portrayed the on-camera persona, but her words were of business and power.

In a society that valued aggressive men and domestic women, Nivens was an aggressive, domestic woman. She was a misfit, yet she approved of society's rules even if they worked against her. She told Mary that "competing with a man is both aggressive and unfeminine";[1] she was blind to the fact that she herself competed in a male-dominated occupation.

If competing with a man was against her code, competing for a man wasn't. In another episode Mary finally addressed Sue Ann's competitiveness and jealousy:

> Mary: Sue Ann, why would you think that I'm interested in snaring Ken? I mean, aren't we past that Sue Ann--the whole idea that women are out to snare men-- I mean, aren't we finally past that notion?[2]

The harpy, of course, was not past snaring men. Her taste for the hunt was her major defining feature. Her zest for conquest, however, competed with her own concept of femininity, and as a result her strategies for seduction were a mix of innuendo and attack. In a scene with Lou, who was always one of her chosen targets, Sue Ann alternately batted her lashes and battled him to the floor:

> Sue Ann: [As they leave the table] What's that expression--a great meal is the prelude to a symphony of lovemaking?
>
> Lou: Who said that?
>
> Sue Ann: I did. [She corners him on the couch

If the harpy failed to find romantic bliss, her career success was a plus, an indication of the ambivalence Americans
were feeling about assertive women in the bedroom and boardroom.   Here the harpy is Sue Ann Nivens (Betty White) of
The Mary Tyler Moore Show with Gavin MacLeod.

wrestling to kiss him.] Go ahead, Lou,
you're stronger than I am, press your
advantage. [3]

Ultimately, the game goes against her; the prize she
sought was lost.   Her aggression bothered others.   Her tidy
apartment of heart pillows and lace could not camouflage the
female predator living within.   Lou told her softly that she
played the wrong role, "The treasure shouldn't do the hunt-
ing, Sue Ann."[4]

Sue Ann Nivens seldom succeeded, in spite of Ted's
description of her as "one hot mama." The harpy on
M*A*S*H wasn't so obvious a failure as a femme fatale,

but then her standards of excellence were considerably lower.   The object of Margaret Houlihan's affections was a weak and passive male, and he was already married.   "Hot Lips" Houlihan, as she was called, was apparently more desperate than even Sue Ann.

Like Sue Ann, Houlihan had a strong sense of the rules--rules by which society operated, rules of propriety and decorum, and military regulations as well.   Her attention to rules and a desire for power were evident in her unbending insistence on the privileges of rank, her complaints about the casual disregard for pomp, and the trappings of rank evinced by other medical personnel.   Her obsession with propriety and regulation could be set aside, however, when it would be to her advantage:

> Hawkeye: Clamp--sponge--Margaret, will you please hand me these things on the beat?
>
> Hot Lips: You're the one that's off.
>
> Hawkeye: Well, let's get together.   Clamp-2-3-4-. Sponge-2-3-4.
>
> Hot Lips: Why can't women lead?[5]

Her desire to lead was great, encouraged by the awareness of her own strength and competence.   Physically, Houlihan was tall, blond, and well-proportioned.   She was athletic and energetic.   She was also strong, as indicated in a scene in which she and a doctor, Trapper, attempted to pry open the medical supply room door.

> Trapper: I'll give you a hand--.   [He attempts but is unable to unjam the door.]
>
> Hot Lips: Let me try.
>
> Trapper: You are strong.
>
> Hot Lips: The way I was raised, every morning we ran naked in the snow.
>
> Trapper: The way I was raised, we ran naked in the subway. [6]

Houlihan's strength and competence led her to expect high performance from others.   As the head nurse of the war hospital, she demanded discipline and strict attention to order and detail.   She was considered a "tough" officer.

She also demanded best effort and positive attitude outside the operating arena, even for team sports.

> B.J.: I know we've lost the last two events, but that's only a temporary set-back. I have every reason to believe that you guys are gonna get out there and win this thing-- Margaret, you wanted to say a few words?
>
> Hot Lips: Thank you, Captain. [Turning to team and shouting] You people stink! You're lazy, you're slow, and you have no spirit. Do B.J. and I have to carry this whole crummy team? Now I want you to get out there and fight. Fight, fight, fight! Let's take it to them! Let's cut out their hearts! Let's win! [Composed again] Thank you, Captain. 7

The contrived intensity of her impassioned appeal to the team demonstrated Houlihan's penchant for artifice and design. She exploited the appearance of passion for her own purposes. Her seduction of Frank Burns, too, was notable for its unspontaneous artifice:

> Hot Lips: Flare your nostrils for me, Frank. I get so excited when you do that.
>
> Frank: I get so excited when you say "excited."8

Houlihan was a graceless enchanter, for her demure manner barely masked her desire to dominate. In her relationship with Burns, she bullied, he whined. She was demanding of him, as with others, but her concern that he excel was founded upon her own interest in power and dominance. Her solicitude was based on strategy; her tenderness born of control:

> Radar: [To Frank] You're being replaced, sir.
>
> Hot Lips: What! This is outrageous. It's completely unfair.
>
> Frank: If you'll excuse me, I'll prepare for the change of command. [Leaves for Houlihan's tent]
>
> Hot Lips: [In her tent, later] Frank, you took that so well. I'm proud of you.

Frank: [Throwing himself on bed, sobbing] Waaa!
              I already wrote Mommy, too.

Hot Lips: Frank, your mother will understand.

Frank: Not my mother. My wife.

Hot Lips: Why you big baby! [Houlihan stomps out,
              leaving Frank who stamps his feet and
              holds his breath, as the scene closes.][9]

Harpy's relationship with a weak male showed her pursuit of her own advantage as exaggerated.   Her single-
mindedness in this pursuit made her intolerant and unbending.
However, Houlihan's obvious competence and her bravery and
dedication to saving lives in the midst of war made her overbearing aggression tolerable.   Her desire to be powerful and
capable in all things was humorous, and, at times, endearing:

[Explosion!]

Hot Lips: Doctor, are you hurt?

Trapper: Just the old football injury....

Hot Lips: We'd better get out of here. [Tries door]
              It won't open! We're trapped--This day's
              been too much. I just can't take it any-
              more! [She cries.]

Trapper: Come on, honey. Take it easy. It's all
              right [hugging her close].

Hot Lips: I'm so embarrassed.

Trapper: Why?

Hot Lips: I outrank you. [10]

The harpy was a character caught in a dilemma.
She advocated male dominance but could not suppress her
need to dominate.   Even though she was aggressive, powerful, competitive, and active, she believed that women should
be none of these things.   She felt men should be the stronger of the sexes, but no one around her was stronger than
she.   She was the kind of man she was seeking.

The man she attracted was naive or weak and effete.
The harpy's misfortune was that her energy and intensity
were not appealing to one who might have been her match.
The passion implied by her reputation as "a hot mama" or

"hot lips" did not evoke passion in a man of equal force. Yet she never gave up the struggle or the search.

For her dedication and her passion she was actually admirable. Her appetite for challenge and her passionate pursuit of her goal were almost heroic. It was only her need of a match and the obvious unsuitability of those that arose that made her a desperate figure, a misfit in the world of maidens and married women. For all that, she wasn't an old maid character vicariously living through the lives of others. It was because she could not accept observer status to life's events that she grabbed at any knight errant who happened along.

More like the traditional old maid character was television's spinster, whose search for a knight errant was marked by a cynical insight as to how unproductive a search it could be. Philosophical resignation was seen in spinster Sally Rogers' retort when Rob Petrie asked if she had heard of Kenneth Dexter: "No. I never went out with a Kenneth Dexter. Of course, a lot of fellows never give their right names."[11] The same resignation and self-depreciation characterized Rhoda Morgenstern in The Mary Tyler Moore Show. When Mary said she had met someone whom she had a strange feeling she would never see again, Rhoda responded: "I know what you mean. I have that feeling on blind dates a lot."[12] Both spinsters bemoaned the pitiful lack of romance in their lives and their inability to alter the situation.

Thus, television's unmarried female was either resigned or rapacious. The harpy's predatory greed distinguished her from the docile spinster who was more to be pitied than feared. Both were obsessed with the matching game; the harpy, however, never gave up hope that her fervor and will would triumph in the end. She was almost glorious in that.

6 ★ THE BITCH

Television women had few moments of glory. As heroes
they were imps, sort of kid sisters to the powerful male
heroes, and as villains, they were generally petty and puny.
Rarely were women portrayed as classic heroes--brilliant,
egocentric peers of the male heroes. Rather, bad women
were manipulative and spiteful, characters who destroyed the
protagonist with little bites and sneaky ploys instead of brilliant strategies and brave blows. In lieu of female villains,
television introduced women as bitches.

The bitch was strong-willed, selfish, and destructive.
Her schemes were self-serving, as were her standards. Often she was without morals or scruples, a sneak and a cheat.
Yet her crimes were minor; she lacked the vision and power
to be truly evil.

Less potent than a villain, she was powerful enough
to cause trouble for someone, usually some male character.
The pawn of her domination was the one closest to her--
husband, lover, or child. Her debilitating and destructive
influence on him was usually evident even to other characters if not to the pawn himself. Her overbearing influence,
her manipulation by guilt or seduction, and her deception
meant anguish for the beleaguered pawn. In crime series
it meant danger for him, too.

Some of the earliest bitch characters were seen on
the crime series. Dragnet showed almost weekly versions
of the bitch manipulating her husband, deceiving her land-
lord, disturbing the peace and police. An episode from the
third season showed the bitch interfering with police work,
by berating the two officers, Friday and Smith:

Woman:	Now why did you have to go and do that?
Friday:	Mam?
Woman:	One thing you men ought to remember--me and my husband are taxpayers.
Friday:	Yes, Mam.
Woman:	We pay your salary. Did you earn your salary today?[1]

The foolishness of her outburst was clear to the audience who knew that she berated the men without cause. She was unaware that they had just risked their own lives to save her son, whose tears she had assumed to be the fault of some police mischief. The irony of the situation increased the absurdity of her tirade.

Dragnet's bitch was intruding, and troublesome, interfering with the important business of crime-fighting and peace-keeping. Yet, she was not opposition but a mere interruption. In spite of the danger her interference posed, as distraction during a shoot-out, Officer Smith and Sergeant Friday dismissed her as a mild annoyance. Neither police officer bothered to explain the situation, treating her with mock politeness instead.

Annoying females came in the guise of mothers, too. Ironside, a later crime series, provided the character of Mrs. Hanson, the middle-aged mother of a young man named Phillip. Again the bitch character was a petty intrusion in the crimefighters' labor:

Mrs. Hanson:	A dating service! Impossible. It's a mistake. Tell them, Phillip.... You've got the wrong man. Phillip wouldn't dream--
Ironside:	Phillip, where were you at one o'clock this morning?
Mrs. Hanson:	He was here with me.
Ironside:	I'm sorry. I asked him, Mrs. Hanson....
Mrs. Hanson:	I know for a fact [that he was here]. As I always do, I went into Phillip's room to tuck him in.
Phillip:	Mother!

<u>Mrs. Hanson:</u>   He's always tossed and turned--ever
since he was a baby. I just made
sure his covers--well, you know how
it is with mothers.

<u>Ironside:</u>   Yes, Mrs. Hanson. I think we do. [2]

We, too, know how it was with the bitch mother.
She was more mother than we cared to see. Her maternal
instinct was grossly distorted, and she was too focused upon
the grown child. She turned her strong will on her child--
guiding him (dominating him) and protecting him from the
perils of the world (the perils of the world's women).

Despite her overmothering, she was not active or dynamic. The bitch mother ruled indirectly, with guilt and
rejection as her tools of persuasion. Her too zealous mothering was a form of passive aggression toward her child.
She manipulated; he capitulated.

In the <u>Ironside</u> episode, Phillip's only transgression
was seeking the services of a dating bureau, yet her shock
and his guilt were evidence that such behavior was not permitted. Like many bitch characters, Mrs. Hanson was hostile toward her son's attempts at self-expression, especially
sexual expression. In most cases, the bitch mother's hostility toward sexuality was not a free-floating feeling but a
direct result of some sexual rejection in her own life. Because she was passive, she avenged her rage on the child.
As possessive and overprotective or cold and rejecting, the
bitch mother enacted a passive response to an ancient
scenario--the woman scorned.

The scenario is a variation of an ancient myth, the
story of Medea. In the Greek myth, Medea, deserted by
her lover Jason, exacted her revenge by destroying his
bride-to-be and murdering their children, avenging on her
children the bitterness and hostility evoked by her lover's
betrayal. The overprotective mother who deprived the child
of life's experience and the cold mother who deprived the
child of love's experience each had her revenge.

The bitch mother scenario appeared in various guises
on dramatic shows of every decade. Examples of the terri-
ble consequences of being reared by a bitch mother were
dissected in detail on medical shows. An episode of <u>Medi-
cal Center</u> entitled "The Betrayal" showcased a bitch mother
named Ellen and Ellen's deprived and disturbed teenage

daughter, Dennie. Dr. Gannon, the series hero, was the
one who discovered that Dennie had had fits since she was
a young child and had been forcibly restrained:

> Gannon: Is that when you locked her up?
>
> Ellen: I kept her from harm, yes.
>
> Gannon: Why didn't you take her to a doctor?
>
> Ellen: Because they'd take her away from me. [3]

As the plot developed, Dennie was taken from Ellen
and Ellen was taken from society.   The story untwisted, re-
vealing that Ellen had kidnapped Dennie from her married
lover in revenge for his betrayal.   Her revenge, like Medea's, was complete, for the child's loss destroyed his wife
and Ellen's pathological overprotectiveness destroyed the
child.

The myth was reflected in the cold and uncaring as
much as the overbearing bitch mother.   A 1975 Marcus
Welby episode concerned an emotionally disturbed child
abandoned by an uncaring mother.   Another character described the mother leaving her child: "She told him to stay
on the steps ... saying she'd be back for him.   I have a
more suitable code name for that woman--Medea. "[4]

The bitch was most damaging as a mother molding a
vulnerable, dependent child.   Yet even then the bitch evoked
none of the terror and awe of the evil.   The scope of her
power was small; her tyranny was confined to her family or
lover.   Her motivation was not malevolence but vanity, self-
interest, or fear.   She was a petty character and if she destroyed others it was not actively and forcefully, but pas-
sively and by omission.

For her passivity and petty tyranny, the bitch appeared
as a bane and a bother even when her concern was more
worldly events.   Pictured in Streets of San Francisco was
such a bitch character, a girlfriend of the young officer
Steve Keller.   The girlfriend, Connie, began to question
the morality of police work and its effects on the officers,
especially Steve:

> Connie: [These criminals] are human beings, Steve,
>   who've been cooped up....   I'm not con-
>   doning violence....   I'm trying to help you.

Steve: Well, you're not helping one bit.

Connie: Don't you feel anything? Is that what being
               a cop is all about? What do you have to
               be--to do that?[5]

Her destructive influence was evident to Steve's partner,
Mike Stone, who tried to argue with her and finally just
told her to stop interfering:

Mike: Connie, you take him or leave him. But
              don't put a monkey wrench between his
              head. Don't make him less than he is.
              And don't get him killed. [6]

The issue she raised--the dehumanizing effect of police work--was lost in the homilies and platitudes with which
she argued her point. Also her choice of subjects for which
to crusade--mass murderers on a rampage--was ill-
considered. Her credibility was further diminished when
her occupation, writing, was revealed to be restricted to a
gourmet column in the Sunday paper. Thus, her confrontation with Keller and Stone was reduced to an uneven match
between an annoying female and two police officers who were
only trying to keep society safe from murderers.

In comedy the bitch was also judgmental and meddling
but she was less objectionable as a character in comic than
in dramatic identification, since comic characters retained a
vulnerability which made their faults seem human weakness
not monstrous aberration. Even so, the fault of being troublesome and interfering was confined to the female of the spe-
cies. Prime among comic prospects of the type was Maude
Findlay of Maude.

Maude was the primary character of a comedy series
which evolved around relations with her husband and neighbors, her daughter, and the family's housekeeper. The humor of the series was in the deceptive appearances and contrasting realities Maude presented as a middle-aged, upper
middle class, liberal bitch. Like every bitch she was selfish, insensitive, and petty, yet Maude was also earnest,
perceptive, lusty, and strong.

Maude was a composite of contrasts. Her self-
absorption contrasted with her crusading vigor to help others
and reform society. Self-absorption also led her to suffer
imagined injustice and indignity, yet be oblivious to the

The humor of the series <u>Maude</u> centered on the contrasting realities Maude Findlay (Bea Arthur) presented as a middle-aged, upper middle class, liberal bitch.   She's shown here with her husband, Walter (Bill Macy).

sensibilities and sensitivities of other people.   She was un-aware of their feelings and of her own effect upon them:

> <u>Maude:</u>   [to housekeeper] Now look, you've got a
> million things to do for the Women's Rights
> Party tonight--you can fix the hors d'oeuvres,
> vacuum the living room, dust the furniture,
> bake the cookies. [7]
>
>   . . .
>
> <u>Maude:</u>   Mrs. Naugatuck, in this house there's no
> such thing as women's work and man's work
> ... women are meant to be more than
> maids, housewives, and sex kittens! [8]

As evident by her insensitivity when telling a housekeeper that women are meant to be more than maids, or another woman to clean the house for a woman's rights party, Maude lacked feeling for other women. She loudly and proudly lobbied for the woman's liberation movement, but Maude herself was not a very liberated woman. She was supportive of women's causes, but she had not a single supportive relationship with another woman. Her daughter was her critic. With her best friend of thirty years she was a rival, a judge, an antagonist:

> Maude: All right, Vivian, I'll talk to Arthur--anything is better than standing here talking to you. [9]
>
> . . .
>
> Vivian: I wouldn't be able to face myself in the mirror.
>
> Maude: With that dress you're wearing, you wouldn't be missing anything. [10]

How Maude acted and her attitude toward other women in the series were more indicative of her character than the causes she espoused or her reasons for doing so. Her insensitivity toward her housekeeper and her animosity toward her friend contrasted with "the woman line" evident in much of the dialogue. Whatever her views, her actions were bitchy. And women were not the only targets of her tongue:

> Walter: Boy, what a great world this would be without women.
>
> Maude: It'd be worth it just to watch you having labor pains. [11]

The bitch was an on-going television type. She appeared in the early days of television and held major roles throughout the first thirty years. In the sixties she began to appear as a mother, and in the seventies comic versions of the bitch mother were shown on the Rhoda series and on That's My Mama.

The bitch was related to the wicked stepmother of fairy tale fame and to the wicked witch of myth and lore. Like them she was strong-willed, destructive, and selfish, but she had none of their force or their power. She was television's vision--meddling, troublesome, sneaky. She was passive and, therefore, a little pathetic.

The most passive of all female character types was the victim.   By definition the part of the victim was passive since
it required no initiative or industry; it simply happened to
the character.   In most cases, it happened to a female character.

In television the role of victim has almost exclusively
been awarded to women.   Even though dramatic shows presented more than twice as many male as female characters
(a seven to three ratio according to most researchers[1]), females were far more likely to be victimized.   Women characters had a 44 percent chance of being a victim in one sample, whereas their male counterparts had only a 25 percent
chance of becoming a victim.   In comic formats both sexes
were victims of circumstance, of their own limitations, or
of capricious authority figures, but comic programs contained few incidences of classic victimization.

The victim, here defined, was a character who suffered pain, disease, imprisonment, or death without in any
way initiating violence or courting danger.   The victim suffered an unwarranted attack or injury.   Injuries involved
falls and accidents, and attacks included assaults on the
body from disease, as well as bullets and blows to the body
by another character.

Identifying the kinds and numbers of acts resulting in
pain, disease, imprisonment, or death to female dramatic
characters was both instructive and depressing.   Victims
were generally one of two kinds, depending upon the type
of program: the medical format showed victims of accident
and disease; action formats (Western and spy-crime) depicted victims of violence.

The victim (here blinded in a stage coach accident) existed only to advertise that the hero, in fact, performed heroically. Sara Lane and John Saxon portray Western versions of victim and hero in <u>The Virginian.</u>

Of the five top-rated dramatic shows of the 1960-61 season only one, Gunsmoke, featured a regular female character. Yet those shows depicted a season of women characters who were robbed, raped, mugged, beaten, kidnapped, and killed. The actions were especially noteworthy since the list did not include any decoy characters (such as policewomen or spies) who courted danger in their profession. Those victims on Rawhide, Wagon Train, Untouchables, Gunsmoke, and Have Gun--Will Travel were innocuous and innocent.

An episode of Streets of San Francisco exemplified the victim circumstances on a typical action show. The episode was appropriately entitled "The Victims." It concerned three escaped convicts who roamed the city, killing and ravaging its citizens. Their first casualty was a clothing store clerk, a young male. Next to die was an old couple, shot to death. These killings occurred in the first twenty minutes of Streets; the remaining forty minutes of the episode dwelt on the fate of a young married couple, the Thompsons.

The Thompsons were surprised in their home by the three escapees. Soon after entering the home, one of the convicts raped Mrs. Thompson in the upstairs bedroom. Then the three abducted her, leaving Doug Thompson to his own devices. Although the killers had warned him not to go to the police, the young husband did anyway, at which point, police officers Stone and Keller began active pursuit of the convicts and their hostage. The police eventually captured the killers and liberated Mrs. Thompson.

"The Victims" episode of Streets was similar in its portrayal of victims to other action shows. Like episodes of Big Town and Big Valley it depicted a sole woman hostage; the portrayal of the female hostage was a particularly helpless image of victim since the woman was totally dependent upon her captors. Like stories on Gunsmoke, Kojak, and Cannon, the victim was eventually rescued by one or more male characters. Even male characters who themselves were captive tried to effect the escape of female hostages. Albert, the old man in the "Victim" episode, echoed the words of numerous other beleaguered male characters in the same situation: "Wait. Wait. Let her go. I don't care what you do to me, but let her go."[2]

The preponderance of female hostages in action scripts reinforced an image of women as vulnerable and

helpless. In no episode the author viewed was a male character a sole hostage, yet women frequently were seen in that
position.   Their vulnerability was openly acknowledged by the
men who sought to protect them from the possibilities of
abuse and assault. The following exchange from an episode
of Big Valley exemplified the dialogue of scores of other
cliché-ridden scenarios:

> Jarrod: Audra, what are you doing here?
>
> Audra: I'm going with you. She's my mother, too.
>
> Jarrod: This is no place for a woman. Kelly, you
>   take Miss Barkley back to the ranch. [3]

The entire outdoors was "no place for a woman" in
many action scripts. Their vulnerability to killing or capture by criminals argued against women engaging in any acts
outside the home. However, they were not safe in their own
homes either, as episodes of Big Town, Dragnet, The Fugi-
tive, Mannix, and Hawaii Five-O graphically demonstrated.

Their vulnerability made women a liability to the men
around them. It seemed as if they attracted trouble. Even
to her captors, a woman was a liability, as argued by two
characters in a Big Valley episode:

> Charlie: If they find this place, we'll have her to
>   blame.
>
> O'Leary: She's nothing but trouble, Jake. We have
>   to get rid of her. [4]

The victim in an action show was seldom a major
character in the story. She had little dialogue and performed
few heroics. She was sometimes nameless; in an episode of
Gunsmoke, a hostage was known simply as "the girl." In
other stories, victim characters were known by their married
names only; in Decoy, a storekeeper who was robbed and
beaten was identified only as "Mrs. Callahan;" in Dragnet a
"Mrs. Anderson" was mugged.

Not only was she insigificant and sometimes anony-
mous in action shows, but she was often the only female
character in the episode. Thus, there were few women
characters other than victim to countermand the image created.   There were scores of active heroes--male characters
--and villains to offset the impression of a few male unfor-
tunates. In "Flannel-Mouthed Gun, " an episode of Bonanza,

The most pernicious television image is that of victim since it has been primarily identified with women.   The prevalence of portraying the victim as female fosters the association of victims with women, thereby projecting an image of helpless, abused women.   Ben Alexander (left) and Jack Webb in a typical victim-scene from Dragnet.

there were ten male speaking characters, not one of whom was subject to unprovoked violence.   The only female character in the episode was a woman identified as "Mrs. Tatum," a victim.

In medical shows the victim was more likely to be a major character in the featured story than she was in an action format.   The victim's circumstances on medical shows differed in other ways as well.   For one thing she had more company.   In eight selected episodes of Dr. Kildare, Marcus Welby, M.D., and Medical Center, there were eight female characters as victim.   She might be a victim of accident or imprisonment, but she seldom suffered physical harm as a direct result of another character's aggression. On medical programs, her injury was generally caused by disease.

The action victim was frequently shot or beaten by a male character. In a Decoy episode, for example, one woman was beaten by her husband and another woman was beaten by a robber. The victim on the medical scene suffered from disease, yet she, too, was sometimes abused by a man. Typically she had fallen in love with a male character who subsequently betrayed her. One example of such a relationship was seen on an episode of Medical Center. Frank Crane explained his dilemma to Dr. Gannon:

> Frank: I never should have come here. It was a big mistake. She thinks--she assumed that I've come here to stay. I'm married. I've got children of my own ... if only she hated me.
>
> Gannon: Give her time, Mr. Crane. I think she'll come around to that. 5

On lots of other episodes of other shows, such as Ben Casey, Medical Center, and Dr. Kildare, the victim suffered heartbreak as well as disease. Like the action victim she was hurt by a man's aggression and power but her vulnerability was emotional not physical. Sometimes the victim suffered her disease--often hysterical paralysis, asthma, or convulsions--as a direct result of betrayal by her beloved. In every case, the victim had fallen in love with a man who was married to another woman. The pattern of disease following transgression made the point that adultery doesn't pay. It doesn't pay for women at any rate.

Other stories dealt with romance in the hospital--doctor-victim relationships were common in these scripts. As the story went, the victim, initially an independent-minded character, resisted the doctor's amorous advances. She subsequently suffered a decline in her physical condition. Episodes of all the popular medical shows contained the story elements described above. A Marcus Welby episode, "Kiley in Love," exemplified the doctor-victim romance. It told of Kiley's attempts to woo Janet Blake and his proposal of marriage on their first date. He was insistent; she was resistant:

> Steve: Marriage is back in. Now it's time to find someone ... how come you never married?

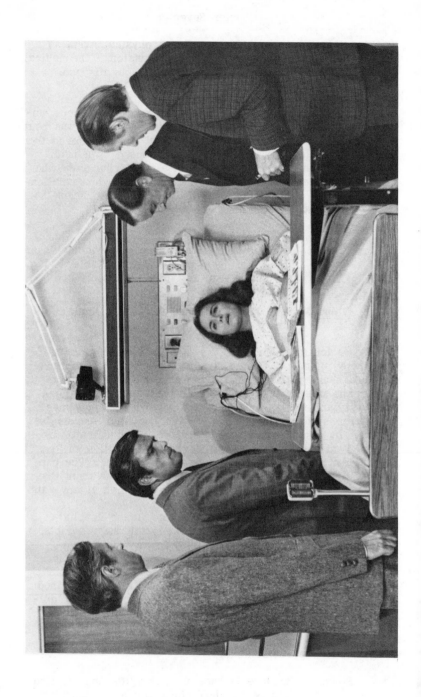

Janet: I have a little black book I keep all the names
          of my discarded lovers....

Steve: I want to marry you....

Janet: You have to know now. There's another man
          in my life--the only man.... You had to go
          and complicate things and I don't need that. 6

Immediately after pronouncing her love for another man,
Janet was thrown from her horse and suffered paralysis
from the waist down. Apparently her cheeky independence
offended the fates or the powers that be. This pattern was
repeated in other shows. *

    The victim was an integral part of most dramatic
shows, yet the story wasn't about her. The story was the
hero's, not the victim's, and for that reason it evolved
around the rescue rather than the effects of the assault.   It
never dealt with the victim's reactions or feelings except in-
asmuch as they revealed her gratitude toward the hero.   The
victim existed only to advertise that the hero, in fact, performed heroically. She was a necessary feature of his role
as mender, defender, redeemer.

    The victim's role as prop for the hero's antics was
not much to write home about but the action show offered
little alternative. For one thing, the place was overwhelmingly populated with men, and men got most of the roles.
Men were rustlers, robbers, extortionists, killers, contrac-
tors, doctors, detectives, lawyers, marshalls, ranchers,

[Opposite:] The most passive of all female character types
was the victim, exemplified by Belinda Montgomery in this
1971 episode of Marcus Welby, M.D.

*The connection between love relationships and disease evi-
dent in both the adultery stories and the doctor-romance
stories suggested a link between the behavior of these wom-
en and their debilitating diseases. On Doctor Kildare, Suzie
spurned Kildare and got leukemia. On Medical Center,
Phoebe rejected her doctor and got breast cancer. Like an
avenging angel, disease struck these characters who did not
love the doctors who loved them. Women seemingly were
"punished" for their sexuality. They were punished for vio-
lating any but the conventional advice offered by a "typical"
Jewish mother--find a nice doctor and get married.

laborers, cowboys, and cartwrights.   Women were wives,
mothers, molls, sisters, and victims.   If a woman wasn't
a victim character she had a few screen moments as some
man's mistress or some man's wife or some man's mother.
By virtue of her gender the female character of action formats had one of two options: to cheer, cherish, feed, and
shelter a male character or to suffer abduction, assault, or
death.   Some people (viewers?) liked to see a woman get
hurt and in a good many cases that was what happened to
her.

On a few action shows there was another female role.
It was a more dominant role than mom-wife-mistress, more
active than victim.   As a role it required woman to embrace
her vulnerability and flaunt it, making it a lure for brutes,
madmen, killers, and pimps.   Being bait was her profession and looking like a victim her primary asset.   She is
discussed in the next chapter.

8 ★ THE DECOY

Looking as weak, appealing, and naive as the victim, the
decoy walked the television streets as bait in chic clothing.
She resembled prey but she acted the hero, for beneath her
painted and pretty exterior she was strong, vibrant and
tough as wood. Many were fooled by her fair frailty. The
evil were undone.

In a typical decoy show, the woman character was
distracted, attracted, and taken captive in short order. The
decoy's part was primary in the first two acts, her partici-
pation less prominent in the capture. She was a hero by intent if not by action.

The decoy shared many qualities with the male hero:
a physical advantage over others, intellectual astuteness, and
a sense of justice and fair play. However, she was also
known by her vulnerability. In that she was uniquely female. She was far more likely than a male hero to be mis-
treated, hurt, or captured. She was frequently caught in
need of rescue. Otherwise, she was conventionally heroic.

The prototype for decoy characters to come was Casey
Jones, a New York policewoman in a 1957 show called Decoy.
Played by Beverly Garland, the character was clever and inventive and incorruptible. She was unique in television programming of the fifties--an urban female hero in a realistic
setting.

In a sample episode of Decoy, Casey Jones showed
herself to be a good cop by finding missing witnesses, inter-
rogating suspects and victims, and speaking Spanish to the
Hispanics. Her credibility as a hero was further enhanced

73

by the voice-overs in which she, like Joe Friday of <u>Dragnet</u>, explained details of the featured crime case. By word and by deed, Jones manifested competence, authority, and courage.

Still, she was vulnerable. Jones took her orders from Lt. Bell, who sometimes sent her to pose as a streetwalker or to go undercover as a reporter--situations in which she could be overpowered or outmaneuvered. She had to be rescued by the lieutenant or other male members of the force more than once in that season of shows.

Because of her vulnerability, the decoy was dependent upon a team or a male superior. In the prototype program she worked with a superior officer. In the sixties, the decoy was always a member of a team or a group, one or more of whom might rescue her. This, too, distinguished her from the male hero, who typically worked alone or with a sidekick, who was a partner or a protégé. Popular action heroes of the period who worked alone were seen on <u>Have Gun--Will Travel</u>, <u>Mr. Lucky</u>, and <u>The Virginian</u>; those who worked with a sidekick included Joe Friday, Matt Dillon, Steve Bailey, and Jeff Spencer. The male heroes who had teams headed those teams: Elliot Ness, Ben Cartwright, and Robert Ironside, for examples. In contrast to the men was the decoy who worked with a team but never commanded it.

The decoy's primary asset to the team was her ability to attract, charm, banter, captivate, fascinate, and beguile. In stories of intrigue her function was to look intriguing. On the <u>Mission Impossible</u> team, for example, in which each team member had a unique capability such as electronics or disguise, Cinnamon Carter's skill was "distraction." It was a term which encompassed the skills of manipulation and seduction, as well as a talent for attraction. Thus in that decade, the decoy added sexual gameplaying to her contributions to the unit to which she belonged.

A representative female member of a crime-fighting unit appeared in the late sixties in the character of Eve Whitfield of <u>Ironside</u>. Her decoy work was featured on several episodes every season. In an episode entitled "Programmed for Danger," Whitfield's work was to pose as a dating service client, attracting the attentions of a strangler who ended relationships abruptly. In "Good Will

On the Mission Impossible team, in which each team member
had a unique capability such as electronics or disguise, decoy Cinnamon Carter's (Barbara Bain) skill was "distraction."

Tour" she escorted a European prince away from incident
and injury in the guise of a society debutante.   In both
stories, her powers of seduction and manipulation were important.   In both she was vulnerable to assault and in need
of rescue by her superior and co-workers.

As decoy, Eve Whitfield was not as heroic as others
of the character-type.   A lower status version of the policewoman on Decoy, Whitfield's professional duties included
making plane reservations and taking phone messages.   She
was a secondary character in a cast which comprised a
black male, a white male, a female decoy, and a white male
chief.   The primary character in Ironside and the series'
hero was the chief.   His analysis and deductions were invariably more astute than the supporting characters.   Whitfield's observations were distorted by "feminine" illogic and
emotionality:

> Eve: You interested in a woman's intuition?
>
> Mark: Where would the world be without it!?
>
> Chief: Probably better off.
>
> Eve: I think he's on the level ...
>
> Chief: Just to convince you what sublime confidence
>   I have in woman's intuition--
>
> Eve: You're gonna be there, too. [1]

Fortunately for Eve Whitfield, the chief was there
later that evening for her intuition had been wrong; the subject of the discussion was strangling her by the throat when
Ironside and the others arrived.   Whitfield's emotionality in-
terfered with her job performance in other episodes in which
she gloated over shopping purchases while being briefed for
an assignment or sympathized with those who subsequently
betrayed the team.

The decoy of the sixties' television seasons was not
as clear-thinking or clever as Casey Jones had been and she
was less prominent in the cast of characters.   She was at
times the team's weakest link.   But what she lost in personal power she gained in fraternal support.   The decoy shows
of the decade contained a family of character types--the
fatherly leader, the older white agent, the brotherly black
agent, the vulnerable and feminine decoy.   Their affection,
their shared experience, and their mutual dependence made
them surrogate family for each other.   It was such a

Eve Whitfield (Barbara Anderson) plays an undercover
role in the "Summer Soldier" episode of <u>Ironside.</u> The
role of decoy was one in which the character was bait
in chic clothing.

satisfactory interrelationship--even for audiences--that it
was duplicated on every successful decoy show (for example,
Mission Impossible, Mod Squad, and Ironside) and even
short-lived shows (Silent Force, Young Rebels, and Girl
from UNCLE) had approximations of the familial structure.
The surrogate family of agents continued on shows of the
next decade.

One seventies series with the familiar combination of
character types highlighted the female agent, Policewoman.
Pepper Anderson of Policewoman more closely resembled
Casey Jones than she did Eve Whitfield.   Like Jones, Anderson was a sergeant in the force, in this case, the Los
Angeles Police Department.   She was likewise blessed with
conventional television hero attributes--good looks, good
health, courage, and craft.

In Anderson's case the "craft" had perceptible emphasis on her ability to attract and encourage a miscellany
of men from pimps to senators.   Men were encouraged by
her sensuality and admiring of her close-fit T-shirts and
low-cut dresses.   Anderson's brassy conviviality gained her
entry into groups she sought to infiltrate.   Seduction, in
short, was her most prominent skill as a policewoman.

But a pretty face and well-shaped waist could not
keep her from harm.   Anderson was frequently victimized
by the criminal groups that she infiltrated.   In one episode,
"The Chasers," she was hit by a truck, dumped from a
moving car, and locked in a closet in a burning room.
Twice in that episode she had to be rescued by her superi-
or, Lt. Bill Crowley.   In another episode, her pose as a
violent revolutionary was unmasked and she had to be rescued by her entire team of co-workers.   She gave them
entry to places they could not easily go; they gave her their
support and brute physical superiority.

However, Anderson received more than artillery
cover and tactical advice from her team of co-workers.
They gave emotional warmth and acceptance, too, providing a sense of community and family that divorcée Anderson did not have in her home life.   Team members Royster
and Styles offered companionship and the solicitous Bill
Crowley offered guidance and reassurance.   Thus, Anderson found in the workplace a strong, family-like team who
would protect and support her.   It was an arrangement
which became increasingly common for prime-time heroes.

Seduction was <u>Policewoman</u> Pepper Anderson's most prominent skill, but Angie Dickinson's pretty face and well-shaped waist could not keep her character from harm.

Two years after <u>Policewoman</u> was introduced, a show
that featured multiple decoys became the hit of the season.
The show, <u>Charlie's Angels,</u> concerned the feats and ventures of three female detectives who took orders from a remote male superior known only as a voice on a phone machine.   They had an associate, as well: a dapper, middle-
aged male who sometimes rescued one of them.   Most often,
however, they rescued each other.   In this they differed
from their predecessors.   Instead of the lone female they
were three and they cherished and defended each other.

They needed defending.   Kelly and Jill (and later
Kris) were exposed, abused, and exploited in various combinations and various ways in episode after episode.   In one
story Kris was rammed by a car, assaulted by three thugs,
and pursued by a murderer.   <u>Angel</u> decoys were so often
tied, jostled, and snatched that they qualified as victims as
well as anyone in the story.   (Sabrina, the other Angel, was
no stranger to danger herself; but after all, she was an imp
character and apparently less helpless.)

Working for Charlie had its down side evidently, but
there was little other work that exercised their training in
sleuthing or their talent for seducing.   The work and the
work setting from the debut episode about a resort caper
typically allowed the trio to gambol in glittery places, ap-
pearing in bikinis and fashion finery.   The accouterments
were assets in their work, for although they had studied
karate and criminology, their chosen resource was usually
provocative attraction.   Jill demonstrated her skill in ma-
neuvers with a character named Ruiz, a tennis pro:

Jill: Can you help me?   Any time you can see me,
        I'm available.

Ruiz: Any time?

Jill: Any time.   Day.   Night.   Afternoon.

Ruiz: Two o'clock.   Lunch?

Jill: Fine.   I'd like that. [2]

Jill's dialogue was specific enough but her body language said more.   With her scanty tennis outfit and her
long, flowing locks, she looked like a model in a lingerie
ad.   The bedroom image was enhanced by her gestures and
movements: swaying walk with the pelvis forward, preen-
ing the hair and lips, prolonged eye contact--signs of female

The decoys in <u>Charlie's Angels</u> were so often tied and jostled and snatched, they qualified as victims as well as anyone in the story.

sexual availability in our culture.   Thus her statement that she was available any time had special significance.

Jill's provocative performance was done to catch a kidnapper.   Scenes like that also captured audiences and therefore subsequent episodes unfailingly featured the physical attributes and seductive techniques of the female detectives.   <u>Charlie's Angels</u> was frequently criticized by tele-

vision analysts for the deliberate exploitation of the three
female characters as sex objects--a justified complaint. It
was also criticized for the poor quality of the acting and the
writing, both of which were inferior to other top-rated shows
of the genre. It had one redeeming feature, however, in
the portrayal of a supportive female group of a popular and
positive character type, the decoy.

Increased evidence of the popularity of the television
type appeared in the next decade, as yet another decoy show,
Hart to Hart, attracted high audience ratings. The decoy
character, Jennifer Hart, was played by Stefanie Powers.
Curiously enough Powers was a third-time decoy, having
tried a sixties and a seventies version of the type in Girl
from UNCLE and Feather and Father Gang, respectively.

Hart to Hart defied convention to some extent by in-
troducing marriage to the world of car chases and covert
action. Jennifer and Jonathan Hart were husband and wife
sleuths in the heritage of The Thin Man but with emphasis
on violence and speed. They alternated their domestic activities with their detective activities, discussing clues as
they sautéed and souffléed, prepared the Brie and chilled
Chablis.

Between teas and tête-à-têtes, the Harts executed
the requisite amount of probes, hunts, feats, stunts, search-
es, and frays. Jennifer Hart was likewise made hostage and
soon redeemed in a requisite number of episodes. Yet the
atmosphere of recklessness and potential violence which the
Harts encouraged merely underscored the security of their
relationship, a marriage marked by veiled passion and a
gentle tenderness usually absent in television matches:

> Jennifer: [rubbing a Buddha-type figure] It's sup-
>   posed to bring you good luck.
>
> Jonathan: If you rub by stomach like that, I'll bring
>   you anything you want. 3
>
>   . . .
>
> Jonathan: We can leave early.
>
> Jennifer: Early? We're getting there late. Why
>   would you want to leave early?
>
> Jonathan: For the same reason we're getting there
>   late. [Exchange of looks]4
>
>   . . .

In <u>Hart to Hart</u> Stefanie Powers was a third-time decoy, having tried a sixties and seventies version of the type in <u>Girl from UNCLE</u> and <u>Feather and Father Gang</u>, respectively.

Jonathan: You wouldn't be leading me down the gar-
            den path?

Jennifer: I certainly would. Especially if it was
            dark enough. [They kiss.]5

For decoy Hart her husband was not only partner and
family but also lover. In previous decoy shows the team
served emotional as well as functional purposes for decoy,
representing both surrogate family and work unit. In this
eighties version, her partner provided physical and emotional support and served as willing companion and inspiration
for her seductive and sexual play.

The seductive decoy was a familiar image but without
the calculated intent of ensnaring the other party her conduct
was charming rather than shrewd. Furthermore, it was
reciprocal, expressing solidarity and mutual attraction more
than one-upmanship. The give and take of sexual promise,
the candor and comradeship evident in their exchanges defined the marriage as multi-faceted and mutually rewarding.

Thus the decoy had evolved to be a more complete
person. Although she still needed rescue at one time or
another, although she tended to provide distraction while
Jonathan provided brute strength, she was more a partner
than a sidekick in their pursuits. Moreover, she was a
partner who was a sexual being with needs, interests, and
desires.

The decoy had become a sexual being without being
a sexual object and she had also found a sexual partner
worthy of her. Perhaps it was the muted appeal of such
healthy sexuality that explained the popularity of the show.
It was popular despite the unimaginative scripts (a characteristic acknowledged even by those connected with the series), and the charm of a lovely and loving decoy was undoubtedly prime among the program's draws.

In Greek mythology, Sirens were female creatures whose tantalizing voices lured mariners to destruction. The television siren shared that capacity for destruction. She was insidiously sexy, harmful yet enticing, and her seduction of a male character led to his eventual demise.

Siren characters included both protagonists and antagonists and the effect on the susceptible male was the same in either case. Antagonists bewitched male heroes and other sympathetic characters. Protagonists seduced villains and rogues.

Seduction was a snap for a certain type who combined a ripe body with a penchant for exhibitionism. Her part in the seduction was only to expose a portion of the leg, wiggle and prance, or push up her breasts when the appropriate party appeared on the scene. For the more active siren, the techniques of seduction were overt, combining verbal advances and come-hither glances. The seduction scenario of a 1958 episode of Maverick showed the siren at work on the hero, Bret Maverick:

> Bret: Mornin'.
>
> Molly: Without even saying 'good'? You can do better than that, can't you?
>
> Bret: Molly, I'm trying to understand you. You're no starry-eyed girl....
>
> Molly: [Kissing him] I have something to show you. Something special.... Will you come?
>
> Bret: I've got too much curiosity not to--and you know it.

<u>Molly:</u> [Kisses him again][1]

The language used by the siren in this episode was
laced with sexual innuendo. Molly's reference to "something to show" and Bret "coming" were sexually suggestive
in the context of her expressions and movements. Her
kisses supported the sexual promise inherent to her speech
and gesture. Ultimately, however, Molly's seduction led to
gunplay, not foreplay.

The siren's seduction led inevitably to destruction on
the frontier. <u>Bonanza</u> gave us graphic example of the fruits
of passion in an uncharacteristically violent episode involv-
ing siren Hallie Shannon. Shannon turned her charms on
three men: the first was shot to death; the second, Lil'
Joe Cartwright, was accused of murder and then critically
wounded by the third; the jealousy and rage of the third
caused him to beat three characters including Shannon herself. The furor over Hallie Shannon's favors diminished
when she fell off a cliff to her death. The sometimes-
suitors who were still alive made peace, and frontier life
presumably resumed.

The intrusive, destructive effect of attractive women,
particularly city women, on the peaceful frontier community
was a frequent thread of Westerns. It was a familiar story-
line of <u>Bonanza</u> where the Ponderosa Ranch offered four
frontier heroes eligible for seduction. <u>Big Valley</u> and the
Barkley Ranch only had three, but siren Hester Converse
did more than enough damage with just the three.

Hester Converse was a full-time siren, a society
debutante from San Francisco. She had mastered no more
taxing endeavors than attending dances and garnering beaux
when she became intent on marrying rancher Nick Barkley.
Jarrod, the most sophisticated of the Barkley men, was the
one who noted that her previous experience ill-fitted her for
rural ranch life: "You know, I can't get the feeling that
this is for you. Stockton isn't exactly San Francisco. The
adjustments to living on a ranch ... to give up the suitors,
the dances, the gifts...."[2]

Without mentioning the satisfaction of multiple seduc-
tions, Jarrod had correctly assessed her tastes and needs.
Converse enjoyed being a practicing siren. She was successful at it. She decided to try being a rancher and since
she could not simply acquire a ranch, she turned her charm
on a rancher and acquired him instead.

Unable to resist a second conquest, Converse turned her demure and helpless demeanor on Heath, another Barkley male. This led to a fight between Heath and Nick, in which Nick was severely injured. The cause of the ruckus was Hester's hopeless weeping on Heath's shoulder when she realized that she would indeed miss "the parties, the dancing, the beautiful clothes." Selfish and irresponsible, the siren used one man's infatuation and another's gallantry for her own purposes.

A key element of the siren's seduction was that the ulterior motives were not only selfish, as Hester has shown, but asexual. The seduction was dispassionate performance. The difference between the harpy and the siren, other than the latter's evident success, was that the harpy meant it and the siren didn't. The siren used her beauty and charm for her own purposes, for material gain, power, favor, but not to express sexual desire or need. Thus her lure was empty promise.

The lure of empty promise was the decoy's hallmark, also, for she played the siren on occasion. At such times she used her skill to catch a thief, a con man or a killer, and then went home and chastely went to bed alone. The average siren, using her charms for her own selfish design, was less philanthropic but no less calculating and unfeeling. Neither seemed to feel a pang or shiver as she roused the chosen male to ardor.

Of course the disappointment of unfulfilled ardor was not the worst result of the siren's skill, for injury and death often followed her kisses and advances. In comic shows her effects were seldom lethal, but financial ruin and ridicule were not unlikely. Her tantalizing appeal was not limited to paramours but apparently extended to television's creators, for the siren was seen in every episodic format in every decade: on The Bob Cummings Show, Gomer Pyle, USMC, and WKRP; on Gunsmoke, Rawhide, and Wild, Wild West; on Dr. Kildare and Rockford Files.

The overall impression promoted by seductive females on television was that sexually expressive women use sexuality to distract, disarm, control, or destroy the male partner. They are dangerous or funny or dangerous and funny. In the siren's case, her overt sexual invitation had harmful results for the male partner and the decoy's lure was a trap for the unsuspecting. The harpy, too, proved detrimental, unmanning the male who came under her influence. All three types

were demonstrably sexual with ultimately negative effects.

Male interactions with the imp, the goodwife, or the
victim were less dangerous but no more satisfactory, for
like most female characters on television, they were basically asexual.   The women who actively pursued men jeopardized the males' freedom, their manhood, and/or their lives.
This pattern had few exceptions, since there were few portrayals of women of normal sexual appetite in active pursuit
of sexual satisfaction.   Without positive sexual females as
alternative images, the portrayal of seductive females told
us that sensual, sexual women are treacherous.

The episodic West was mostly a male preserve. Women who wandered onto the frontier, like Molly and Hallie and Hester, were soon removed--to prison, to the grave, or to the city. Except for the imp, the only woman in the West who didn't find the frontier a hostile place was the courtesan.

The courtesan was an unconventional woman, an entrepreneur whose satin skirts and saucy tongue suggested a prostitute. Perhaps she was also a prostitute, but, if so, it wasn't revealed on network television. What was revealed was a saloon keeper or cabaret hostess, an impudent female who was self-supporting and sexually appealing.

She was a safe target of sexual fantasy, for her easy familiarity with men's ways not only made her unlikely to rebuff advances but it rendered her unfit for marriage, and therefore incapable of trapping an unwary male. Her safe accessibility appealed to more than one frontier hero. Lily Merrill of Lawman, Nellie Cushman on The Life and Legend of Wyatt Earp, and the preeminent Kitty Russell of Gunsmoke provided the hero's love interest in their respective series.

Gunsmoke provided maximum opportunity to see the courtesan and the hero in the twenty-year romance of Kitty and hero Matt Dillon. Matt and Kitty's relationship was one of equal beings with different styles: she, strong-willed and worldly-wise, was practical and business-minded; he, sincere and tolerant, was also iron-willed and idealistic. She discussed the business with him and he discussed peace-keeping and law-breaking with her. They were enormously self-sufficient yet supportive of one another:

Kitty: [Observing Matt pacing as she pours after-dinner brandy] What is it, Matt?

Matt: You've heard me speak of Adam Kimbro?

Kitty: So many times I can give you chapter and verse....

Matt: He's in trouble.... I gotta do something, Kitty.

Kitty: Of course you do. Because [pause] maybe you can see yourself in him.

Matt: You know something? There's times when a woman can be too smart for her own good-- even if she is a good cook.

Kitty: Go on, get out of here. Go find him. You're not good to anyone until you do. [1]

How good he was when Matt wasn't worried about Adam Kimbro remained unexplored, but generally there seemed to be no heavy breathing in this romance. Matt,

Courtesan Kitty Russell (Amanda Blake) of Gunsmoke was an entrepreneur, distinguished from domestic pleasers of men as much by her unmarried independence as by her painted face and peacock feathers.

at least, resisted intimacy, even the implied intimacy of
sensitive insight, and so they responded to one another with
affection marked only by smiles and looks.   They had none
of the fervor and passion the Harts displayed.   Or they had
exquisite discretion.

The soul of discretion and the heart of the mercenary
coexist in Maverick's courtesan, Samantha Crawford.   Maverick was a spoof of Westerns and Crawford contributed to
the satire.   If courtesan combined commerce and crinolines,
Crawford was the parody, affecting the delicate air while ef-
fecting the artful dodge.   She was the hero's equal, and
since Maverick was the quintessential rogue, she matched
him ruse for ruse.

She was a charming charlatan, a picture which was
paraded in full regalia on a 1958 episode entitled "According to Hoyle."   The episode concerned Bret Maverick's uneasy alliance with Crawford, a professional gambler like
himself.   Maverick proposed the partnership but it was her
assets rather than her abilities which motivated him, for
Crawford was, he claimed, "one of the worst [poker play-
ers] ever seen."[2]

Samantha Crawford's shill was manipulation of people, not cards.   Her feigned Southern accent and pretended
delicacy were contrived to charm the unsuspecting.   With
calculated single-mindedness she not only charmed but
cheated her associates.   In "Hoyle" she double-crossed
her two previous partners by forming an alliance with Maverick, and subsequently double-crossed him, leading him to
observe, "Samantha, you just proved something my old pappy used to say, 'Man's the only animal you can skin more
than once.'"[3]

She proved she was not what she seemed.   She looked
delicate and weak, hiding a strong will and a healthy consti-
tution which even a hot, bumpy stagecoach odyssey did not
diminish.   Her helplessness was a ploy, a bluff upon which
her success as a gambler and entrepreneur was based.   As
she said of a winning card gambit--"only a woman could
have pulled that trick and made it work."[4]

Samantha Crawford was not unsympathetic in spite of
her guile and perfidy.   She was likable because she was vulnerable herself, a fox in wolves' company.   She was a
Southern lady who was neither highborn nor Southern, amid
gentlemen who were cutthroats and thieves.   In the wild and

perilous West, her pretensions were merely natural protec-
tion, intended, like the chameleon's coloring, to camouflage
her presence in an alien environs.

The courtesan lived in a man's world but she differed
from other types who also did.   Unlike the victim she had
her own resources and planned her own defenses.   Unlike
the imp she used the accouterments of her sex--the paint,
satin, and feathers--to attract her allies.   She cultivated
men as allies not as conquests.

It was a different purpose from that of the decoy and
the siren, who caught his eye to catch the man.   Sexual attractiveness was her coin in trade, yet courtesan did not ex-
ploit her admirers.   For one thing, pleasing men was not a
pastime but a job for her and the means by which she main-
tained her own autonomy in a male-dominated place.

Her success was attested to by her ability to survive,
even thrive, in a masculine world with male mentors and
friends to support her.   Her acceptance was based in part
on her ability to look frail and get the job done.   If she
overstated her feminine stance, her lack of subtlety appealed to men who were equally direct in their sexual trappings, to the gunmen and lawmen of the West and later to
the truck drivers, cowboys of the contemporary settings.

One such contemporary courtesan was Flo, the truck-
er's delight on Alice (and subsequently on Flo).   Her appeal
to men was the stuff of legend and evidently her vocation in
life.   She herself provided the most explicit description of
courtesan in action:

> Flo: I was sitting in the bar at the Chez Chug-
> a-Lug, just lightening it up with the crowd,
> telling jokes and screaming around, you
> know and this guy ... said he'd never seen
> anybody handle men and draw a crowd the
> way that I do.   And he offered me a job
> as his head hostess in Houston. [5]

The courtesan's "handling" of men was essentially benign.   She genuinely liked men and they liked her for it.
Flo, in fact, was brazen in her appreciation:

> Flo: How'm I gonna pay you guys back?

The hussy with her frankhearted manner and blatant appeal was part of the courtesan. Flo's overstated accouterment--the coronet of curls, dangling earrings, and down-home drawl-- showed her hussy side.

Ralph: You'll think of a way. [Exchange of looks]
            I just came by for a goodbye kiss.

Other
Truckers: I'd like to have a goodbye kiss, too.   Me,
            too.

Flo: Well, if you guys got the lips, I got the
            pucker. 6

It was the hussy who appealed to them.   The hussy
with her frankhearted manner and blatant apparel was part
of the courtesan.   Flo's overstated accouterments--the
coronet of curls, dangling earrings and down-home drawl--
showed her hussy side.   They said she was accessible,
warm, and sexually unthreatening.

For all her safe accessibility, the courtesan was
more than a whore with a heart of gold.   In her manner and
speech she showed a fine and forthright appreciation of her
own worth, an attitude which prevented her from being imposed upon or abused.   Flo's reply to imposition or criticism was "Kiss my grits."   Kitty's was slightly more subtle:

Bull: You're the hardheadest woman I think I
            ever met.

Kitty: Thank you. 7

Neither retort left any doubt about the courtesan's
own estimation of herself.   She enjoyed herself, her work,
and the position in which she found herself.   Sometimes she
was aware of the fringe benefits, too, as Flo observed (while
modeling a ring from an admirer), "You don't get this for
good behavior."8

Sometimes the courtesan gave the impression that she could take advantage of men but that she chose not to do so. The witch left no doubt about her power over men and her inclination to use it. Every witch saga focused upon her power and the difficulties it presented for the man who had to live with her. For some reason, usually male pride or the pretense of custom, the male always insisted that the witch curtail and conceal her power and act like a housewife. Invariably she struggled to do so, even as she covertly resisted domination and restriction by using her power to get her way. (Actually, witch series were not the only shows of the sixties to reflect women's rejection of the housewife role. Women who had difficulty enacting the role that had been so pervasive on television the previous decade were also seen on Please Don't Eat the Daisies, Green Acres, Pistols and Petticoats, and The Debbie Reynolds Show.)

Her special power varied in every witch saga. On Mona McCluskey and Love on a Rooftop the woman's power was her extraordinary wealth. On most witch series, however (such as I Dream of Jeannie, My Living Doll, Bewitched, The Girl with Something Extra) her power was supernatural: witchcraft.

Witchcraft as particularly female is an ancient association, carefully documented.[1] Historically, the source of this female power was rooted in a sisterly network or coven of women whose knowledge of herbs and potions, words and poisons gave them power over others. The image was essentially domestic--women in dark smocks with brooms and pots of bubbling brews. Even in the sanitized and streamlined sets of prime time, the basic elements remained: the sisterhood of witches and the domesticity of their image.

The sisterhood was represented in the attentions and favors exchanged among women, as they advised and assisted each other.   The actual activities of the sisterhood were decidedly domestic.   Esmeralda of <u>Bewitched</u> practiced her witchcraft in the kitchen mostly, serving as supernatural maid and cook for the Stevens family.   Samantha Stevens and other witches on the series made canapés, as well as potions and antidotes.   Rhoda Miller of <u>My Living Doll</u> and Jeannie on <u>I Dream of Jeannie</u> served food and entertained guests.   Thus, the witch mixed her magic and, in typical television manner, she also cooked and kept a tidy house for Bob or Mike or Tony.   An ideal example of the saga could be seen on the series <u>Bewitched,</u> in which Samantha Stevens was a witch.

An episode entitled "Man or a Mouse" concerned Samantha's efforts to counter a spell which threatened to change Darrin into a mouse by midnight.   Endora, Samantha's witch-mother, had cast the spell on Darrin to express her annoyance and jealousy.   Against this plot was the office story about the exceptional security measures instituted by Darrin's boss to safeguard ad proposals for the Illinois Meat Packers Association.   The proposals disappeared and Darrin was suspected until a lucky circumstance saved the day.

In another sample episode Samantha's family again proved threatening, when Maurice, Samantha's father, paid a surprise visit to see his namesake, the newborn grandson. He was stunned to discover that the child was named for Darrin's father, not him.   Maurice was a powerful warlock and his subsequent anger sounded thunder and broke lamps and vases; it also caused him to cast a spell trapping Darrin in an entry hall mirror.   The satisfactory conclusion of this episode resulted from Samantha's abilities to outwit the warlock.

Samantha's power over people included that which was supernatural.   Her ability and that of other superhumans in the show to cast spells, create illusions, transcend space, and make seven-course meals materialize instantly besotted and amazed the mortals in residence.   Even the enlightened and resistant Darrin was susceptible to Samantha's magic.

The spellbinding enchantment of Samantha's witchery was mysterious, but it was not sinister.   Endora, on the other hand, portrayed the dark side of witchery, the physical

and spiritual opposite of the good witch.   She was like a
classic mother-in-law joke: meddling and malicious, using
her powers to unman her daughter's husband.   In the
"Mouse" episode she literally transformed a man into a
mouse, and only Samantha's trickery kept it from being
Darrin.

Darrin's mistrust of Endora and her powers would
seem to have been well-founded but his discomfort with
Samantha's use of witchcraft was less understandable.   His
insistence that she relinquish her powers of witchcraft and
observe natural, "manmade" rules of behavior suggested an
aversion to being dominated by her, even with positive results.   In fact, there were indications that he was dominated
by her.   She was politely insistent in events concerning magic
and its antidote:

Samantha: Sweetheart, it's almost midnight.

Darrin: Oh, yes, bewitching hour.   Okay, where
           do you want me?

Samantha: In the kitchen.   I'll get rid of her as soon
           as I can....

Darrin: You're sure that antidote of yours will
           work?

Samantha: Positive.

Darrin: Well, if it doesn't, remember to get rid
           of the mousetraps. [2]

Samantha's dominance was exercised only in her own
sphere of influence, the affairs of her immediate family.
She had neither interest nor expertise in the worldly affairs
which concerned men and she managed to make them appear
as foolish, if harmless, pursuits.   She commented about
her husband's percentage of the Meat Packers account, "Oh
that's wonderful, Sweetheart....   And I hope the Meat Packers win every game they play this season."[3]

Equating the Meat Packers Association with a sports
team was a social gaff but it subtly suggested that male
concerns were merely games.   The male domain existed in
the military or professional world where men obeyed the
rules and sought a common boon like players on a team.
By contrast, the female domain, though strictly domestic,
was practical and immediate, concerned with the personal.
The major conflict of witch sagas was the struggle for

dominance between the male and female domains. It was a struggle in which the man looked the fool and the woman a schemer and a sneak.

Yet there were men who weren't game players. They were potent forces in the world, unencumbered by convention and social ties. They were unmarried.

Maurice, the warlock, was such a man. His name was uttered with respect by both Endora and Samantha and in the flesh he was awesome. Whereas Endora's arrival was heralded with the tinkling of a bell, Maurice's appearance was preceded by thunder. When he appeared, it was in a mantle of dark clouds and he spoke in a voice of great resonance. His magic, too, was more potent than Samantha's attempts to neutralize it. Samantha, however, would counter with charm and trickery, accomplishing by manipulation what she could not in direct confrontation.

In numerous instances, the witch favored cajoling and manipulation although more imposing powers were hers to command. She bullied, charmed, and coaxed other characters to do her bidding. Her manipulation of Darrin was transparent in a scene in which she convinced him to drive her to a heliport:

> Samantha: Isn't there a helicopter service from this town to the airport?
>
> Darrin: Yes. But--
>
> Samantha: Honey, that's a great idea![4]

It was a typical witch trick encountered in every witch series, but there was probably no more blatant manipulation than that seen in I Dream of Jeannie. That series explored new parameters of feminine deception and manipulation as it recorded its story of an astronaut's attempts to adjust to life with a genie. The genie, artfully named Jeannie, dissembled, dissuaded, pleaded, and provoked to get her way. When all else failed she used magic:

> Jeannie: Please let me go with you, Master. Please.
>
> Tony: No, this is men's work....
>
> Roger: Boy, you sure know how to handle her.

For women audience members, the superhuman capabilities of the witches and genies on situation comedies of the 1960's were a reflection of both fantasy and frustration. I Dream of Jeannie exemplified the witch's use of deception and manipulation, with Barbara Eden in the title role.

> Tony: You gotta be firm.
>
>   [Meanwhile, Jeannie, mocking masculine
>   imperatives, has reduced her size and
>   slipped into Tony's pocket.]5

Witch series like I Dream of Jeannie and Bewitched
were rooted in the improbable and the absurd, of course,
but their importance as expression of the period cannot be
dismissed for those qualities.   Absurdity and improbability
buttressed many comic series and the fantasy underlying
these conventions revealed attitudes and values which might
have been repressed otherwise.   The timely popularity of
witch stories suggested that the fantasy had profound significance for the mid-sixties.

In witch sagas the fantasy disguised a male-female
struggle.   It was one in which the male had custom and
authority on his side but one which he invariably lost anyway since his career as a military or professional man was
compromised, or even jeopardized, by the witch's actions.
For her part, the witch was merely experiencing a sense of
her own power.   Like the fifties' imp she implicitly rejected
the secondary status of her role as wife, but, unlike Lucy
or the others, she had the power to alter the consequences.
Unfettered with the limitations imposed on the imp of the
fifties, the witch reflected her time.

The depiction of her subtle rejection of her secondary
status and of the sisterhood who supported her was appropriate to a decade of feminine protest and affiliation.   But
the covert aspect of her rebellion and her penchant for manipulation and deceit meant that her actions were not quite
acceptable to the American public.   She was a sixties figure,
to be sure, but her avoidance and deception kept her from
being a hero.   Nevertheless, in portraying an independent
character, a woman with a sense of her own power, she
prefigured the women of the decade to come--women who
were not character types but unique and wonderful characters unto themselves: Mary Richards of The Mary Tyler
Moore Show, Kate Lawrence of Family, Billie Newman and
Margaret Pynchon of Lou Grant, and Elaine Nardo of Taxi.

The surprising power or authority of a few women characters of the night realm made them fascinating if rare. The
witch was one such type with undeniable power. The matriarch was another and she had prestige as well as power.

She was a queenly sort whose power arose as much
from her personality as circumstance. She was past life's
prime and could use the stature of age to influence others,
yet she was never annoying or cranky. She was two or three
times as old as the imp, the goodwife, or the siren; an infrequent image in television; and one who was noteworthy for
her positive characteristics.

The matriarch was frankly heroic: prominent, competent, forceful and courageous. When in peril, as she was
so often in adventure programs, she showed her mettle and
spunk. Her prestige in her community arose from such
characteristics, as well as from the power and status attributed to her.

She was powerful in the lives of other characters.
Like any leader, her power was of two types--social and
actual. Social power, influence based upon promise of social favors or the threat of disapproval, was the typical
power exercised by matriarch. It was demonstrated by
words or gestures that suggested her approval or disapproval of some action by a family or group member. The
member's compliance or defiance testified to the matriarch's
power. A matriarch figure on Maverick showed her strength
in Bret's behalf:

Ma: Hold on. This here's a friend of mine. [To

101

the crowded saloon] Boys, can't a friend of
mine play if he wants to?

<u>All</u>:   YEAH ! ! ! ![1]

Less common than demonstrations of social power
was the exercise of actual power by a matriarch character.
Actual power, those decisions which affected the awarding
of resources to others, was determined by roles seldom
awarded to female characters.   Resources (including land,
money, medicine, and personal freedom) were distributed
by those enacting roles as government agents, generals,
sheriffs, employers, doctors, lawyers, judges, and mayors.
The only actual power demonstrated by female characters
was likely to be in the role of mother of small children.
Nevertheless, there were exceptions, and some matriarchs
demonstrated actual power, as well as social power, over
a family, community, or group.

The matriarch differed from male heroes in at least
two characteristics: her domesticity and her vulnerability.
Her domesticity was revealed in the actions and setting
typically associated with her.   Although she may have been
a mayor, rancher, or robber, her actions frequently concerned domestic chores--preparing or serving food and coffee, planning or executing social functions in her home.   Her
setting was usually the home.   Furthermore, she was frequently a matriarch in the conventional sense--the mother
of a large, powerful family.   Thus, her domesticity was an
important characteristic; her association with family and
home was an attribute of her personality.   The association
of domesticity with positive female characteristics has been
discussed in relation to other female character types, particularly in situation comedy.   The association of domesticity with "good" female characters is a subject which will be
discussed in the next chapter.

The second characteristic of the matriarch which distinguished her from similar male characters was her vulnerability.   Matriarch characters were vulnerable to being victimized.   They suffered illness, accidents, kidnapping, and
betrayal far more frequently than males.   Even those males
ostensibly more vulnerable than powerful women--young boys
and impoverished old men--were less subject to being victimized than were matriarchs.   It was a pattern in dramatic
programs particularly, which was oft-repeated with female
characters.

Big Valley's Victoria Barkley, portrayed by Barbara
Stanwyck, presented a typical matriarch. The character,
mother of four grown offspring, owned Barkley Ranch, a
prosperous cattle ranch in California's San Joaquin Valley
in the 1800's. Victoria was prominent and powerful, dis-
playing all of the matriarch characteristics described above.

Victoria's power and status in the community were
evident from declarations by other characters. In one episode, a character exclaimed, "Mrs. Barkley! Queen Bee
of the whole valley!"[2] In another episode, an outlaw observed, "From the looks of her, she's a high-flown lady."[3]

Matriarch Victoria's power and influence over others
arose not only from the actual power inherent to her position
as ranch owner, but from social power ascribed to her. In
an episode entitled "Teacher of Outlaws," the outlaw's ad-
miration for her spunk led him to note, "It's been a long
time since I took orders from a lady."[4] In another episode,
"Fall of a Hero," Victoria was depicted as persuasive with
her lawyer son Jarrod. The judge in a case Jarrod was
pleading appealed to Victoria's influence with her son: "Get
him off the case, Victoria. I don't care how you do it, but
do it."[5] Typically, Victoria's influence was appeal and persuasion. Thus, despite the title "Queen Bee of the whole
valley," Victoria's power was primarily the social power
dependent upon personality characteristics.

Victoria Barkley's personality traits were those characteristic of male heroes: courage, daring, intelligence, and
integrity. In "Teacher of Outlaws," Victoria displayed courage and spunk in a bad situation: capture by a band of robbers. The outlaw leader commended her, "you don't scare
easy."[6] Furthermore, she assisted the captive doctor in his
escape from the band. In another episode she helped a
wounded man escape from gunfire:

Jason: You stay here undercover.

Victoria: No, I'm going with you. You'll need help.
            Do you think you can mount?

Jason: Yes.

Victoria: [Running] Don't you start until I draw
            their fire. [7]

In spite of her resourcefulness and courage, she was

not infrequently a victim. In the "Teacher" episode, she
was kidnapped by outlaws and in evident danger from injury
or rape. One outlaw leered at her as he said, "A pretty
girl gives a man an appetite."[8] Although she managed the
doctor's safe escape in that episode, she was unable to effect her own and had to be rescued by the posse, an all-
male group, among which were her own sons.

          In another episode, entitled "Presumed Dead," Vic-
toria was again a victim in need of rescue. As a result of
a stage coach accident in which she was injured, she suffered amnesia. Rescued by a cattle rustler who wanted her
for his wife, she was again in the company of menacing outlaws: "She's nothing but trouble, Jase. We'll have to get
rid of her."[9]

          When she was not depicted as a victim of illness,
accident, or violence, she seemed to be little in evidence.
Although a central character, her roles seemed limited to
peripheral actions in those episodes which did not involve
her in some vulnerable situation. In two episodes selected
randomly for analysis, "By Fires Unseen" and "Fall of a
Hero," Victoria was neither predominant nor heroic. In the
latter episode, her actions were mostly limited to reactions
to the behavior of two of her sons, Jarrod and Heath. Her
dialogue primarily consisted of domestic concerns: "Maybe
we ought to invite him to dinner"; "Aren't you going to eat
your breakfast?"[10]

          In the episode entitled "By Fires Unseen," Victoria
was more evident and her authority over her children was
demonstrated. She told her daughter Audra, "You're not
going to the station dressed like that!" On a family excur-
sion in which Nick was hurt, she was evidently in charge:
"We'll set up camp here. You hurry back." In that episode, however, her primary image was that of mother, not
matriarch. Her concerns were the sibling rivalry among
her sons and that Nick not make an unsuitable marriage.
Her dialogue was sprinkled with domestic anecdotes and advice to Nick's intended: "I'm going to teach you to make
the best Western breakfast in the whole world."[11]

          Matriarch, as portrayed by Victoria Barkley was,
therefore, distinctly domestic. Her concerns were the wel-
fare of others, but particularly the members of her own
family. Her actions were sometimes independent activities,
such as horseback riding or reading, but more frequently

consisted of offering food and drink and ministering to the sick and wounded.   It was a positive image although stereotypically feminine in many ways.   In one episode a male character described Victoria as "kinda strong-like, but soft, too, and gentle. "12

Bonanza of the same era showed us one less gentle but every bit as "strong-like."   Ma Reichman, mother of three ruffian males, was slightly less respectable than Victoria Barkley but no less respected.   Her sons obeyed her; the townspeople respected her, if only for her grit and her gun.   Hoss, that intimidating Cartwright giant, came to respect her, too:

> Ma: You think I'm gonna turn over one of my boys to you?   Or to anybody else, you are wrong, Mister.   Your case is a bottle short.

> Hoss: Ma'am, why don't we let the court decide that?

> Ma: Strange court in a strange town?   With the judge scratching the sheriff's back and the sheriff scratching the judge's back?   They're both up for election and the local people are breathin' down their necks?   Man would have a fine chance in court like that.   Besides in my opinion, this ain't much of a crime; my boys are young and they're feisty and they're a little bit rougher than most but they ain't criminals.   This meeting's adjourned. 13

And so it was.   Against great odds such women prevailed.   Great odds seemed even to produce them for they sprang from the frontier's unfriendly soil and the homespun hardships of rural regions.   Besides the frontier women discussed above were rural matriarchs Granny Moses of The Beverly Hillbillies and Kate Bradley of Petticoat Junction.   A seventies edition appeared on Charlie's Angels as character Lydia Danvers, again in a rural setting.

Lydia Danvers was the mayor of a small town and a woman much like Victoria Barkley.   She was in her fifties or sixties, competent and intelligent.   By virtue of her position as mayor, she had power and prestige.   She was also courageous, as evident in the excerpt in which Kris, Sabrina and Bosley discussed their plan to save hostages:

> Kris: O. K. , Aunt Lydia, you stay here, and Bosley, if it goes down, you get her out of here.

Bosley: I will.

Lydia: No, he won't. I'm going with you.

Kris: I'm sorry--under no circumstances. I want
          you up here where it's safe. I'm sorry,
          it's just too dangerous for you.

Lydia: Why, because I'm too old?

Kris: I didn't say that.

Lydia: Well, you didn't have to. They're my
          friends and my husband is there. I can't
          do any less than my best for them. I have
          to take as much risk as they're taking. If
          I don't, then I'm as old and helpless as you
          seem to think I am.... We're wasting time.

Sabrina: Let's go![14]

Lydia Danvers was competent as well as courageous.
Not only did she risk her life for her community, but she
also succeeded in assisting in the release of her captive
husband and friends. Her competence was due to her control and also to her ability to coerce and cajole. As she
stated it, "I never saw a man I couldn't handle yet."

Other than calming the captive hostages and cajoling
the kidnapper, Lydia's activities were more mundane than
municipal. Her image was domestic. As mayor, she was
depicted serving coffee while conferring with the town leaders in her living room. Except for the rescue scene, she
was always seen in her own home or front yard. The domesticity of her image, however, could not diminish the
drama of the confrontation scene when she said, "I can't do
any less than my best for them," spoken like a hero.

PART IV

★

CONCLUSIONS

13 ★ IMPLICATIONS AND INCRIMINATIONS

Television's ladies of the evening have been arrant distortions of American womanhood. Of course, television content is popular art and some distortion of reality can be attributed to poetic license. Irony, hyperbole, and caricature are core to the definition of situation comedy, just as conflict and pathos are to dramatic genres. Nevertheless, television failed to accurately represent women by even the grossest measures: the ratio of female to male characters greatly overrepresented males and the ratio actually decreased over the thirty-year period. (The male-female ratio of the twenty highest rated programs of the 1980 season was approximately 7 to 3, whereas males outnumbered females only 6 to 4 in the most popular shows of the first network season.)

Concentrating on the female characters has exaggerated their relative visibility in prime time. In reality the incidence of featured females like Lucy, Samantha, and Flo was uncommon in television fare. Series that did feature women included prominent male characters, too, yet many male-centered series had no female characters. There were formats that presented womanless worlds for a decade at a time. Westerns, military tales, and detective series showed such worlds.

In the fifteen most popular Westerns between 1955 and 1965 only <u>Lawman,</u> <u>Gunsmoke,</u> and <u>Wyatt Earp</u> had regular female characters. Some heroes, like <u>Cheyenne</u>'s character, like Paladin of <u>Have Gun--Will Travel,</u> and Vint Bonner of <u>Restless Gun,</u> were loners, men with violent pasts which made them misfits in civilized communities. Others, like <u>Bonanza</u>'s patriarch, Ben Cartwright, and <u>Rifleman</u>'s Lucas McCain, were widowers with motherless sons. The impression effected by such composition was the West as a community of men.

During the same period twenty-two military comedies and dramas premiered on prime time, only five of which had any regular female characters. In detective series, too, women were scarce: out of seventeen series, six contained regular female roles. When women were included, they were likely to be weak or foolish.

In many of these series women were victims--weak, helpless, sometimes in desperate need of rescue. In other series women were characters like the courtesan or the harpy, who spent their lives in the futile pursuit of heroic men. Over time it was obvious that a hero's interest in a woman was transitory; his real interests were his work and other men. Yet women characters were interested in him or in other uncommitted men, a situation which trivialized them and made them look foolish.

On situation comedy, men, particularly fathers, sometimes played the fool, but the male sex was not presented as foolish since the bumbling, befuddled male figure was balanced with male characters who were capable, reasonable, sometimes powerful. Examples of capable male foils to the bumbling fathers were found in The Life of Riley, as Jim Gillis and Riley's boss; Ozzie's older son in The Adventures of Ozzie and Harriet; and Maurice and Larry Tate in Bewitched. Furthermore, capable fathers were seen on scores of popular shows of the same period, including Father Knows Best, The Donna Reed Show, Leave It to Beaver, The Beverly Hillbillies, and My Three Sons.

The image of women as weak or foolish was highlighted by their scarcity in Western, military, and detective series. In some episodes of these shows the only female character, surrounded by a variety of male characters, was a victim. In others the female role was largely ornamental, like that of the leggy, faceless "Sam" of Richard Diamond.

Women who were visible whether only as legs or as prominent, dominant characters were viewed from a male perspective. They were seen in juxtaposition to a male as a wife, lover, ally, foe, or mother. And, as such, they were good or bad. The goodwife (the contented homemaker) contrasted with the rebellious, rowdy imp and with the aggressive harpy. The image of the courtesan was good, op-

posing that of the siren who was dangerous.   The matriarch
contrasted with bitch.   Three types--victim, decoy, and
witch--were on the edge, with the potential to be good or
bad, and they appeared in stories that addressed that con-
trariety.   All were seen in relation to men as safe, controlled, or capricious, and as enchanting or destructive.
From this perspective what was female was paragon or
prostitute, angel or devil.   The female character did not
represent a human being struggling with good and evil but
rather she represented an embodiment of good or evil.

There were many instances of this dichotomy of images every television season in every episodic format.   The
goodwife, seen as Harriet Nelson, Diane Walker, Laura
Petrie, and Edith Bunker, was always a character who was
virtuous, tolerant, submissive, sensible.   She was consoling and nurturant to her husband, seldom a source of distraction or distress for she was family-centered, competent
and contented with the management of the home.   If she was
sometimes fussy, concerned with petty affairs, her complaints were familiar and predictable.   She was domesti-
cated, under control.

Her contrast was the impulsive Lucy Ricardo, Laverne De Fazio, Cal (Calamity Jane), or Elly Mae Clampett,
the imp who was inept as a homemaker, unable to adapt to
the domestic role.   Whereas the imp was active and rebellious, the goodwife was contented, even passive in her acceptance of her secondary status.   She was dependent and the
imp was vigorously independent.   She was selfless and the
imp was the center of her universe.

For these submissive, selfless, dependent traits, the
goodwife was distinguished from the harpy, too.   The intrep-
id and intolerant harpy was anything but selfless.   Although
she longed for goodwife's marital bonds, she was as wildly
unsuited for such a union as one could be.   The harpy, as
Sue Ann Nivens or Hot Lips Houlihan, was controlling with
men; her domineering aggression was the opposite of the
goodwife's submission.

Paired opposites were also seen in the courtesan's
safe accessibility and the siren's dangerous enticement and
in the powerful matriarch and the petty, debilitating bitch.
When the matriarch was a mother, she was courageous and
giving; the bitch mother was intrusive, sneaky, and selfish.
Such contrasts portrayed a picture of women as a good-bad
dichotomy.

Like other witch series, the comedy <u>Bewitched</u> depicted both sides of the dichotomy and the conflict of witch characters was between two competing but opposing images. Characters Endora and Serena clearly represented malevolent sorcerers. They were magical, enchanting, and dangerous to mortal men. Like imp characters, they were impulsive and independent, out of man's control. Samantha Stevens, as a superhuman, had the same power that they did; she, too, was magical and charming. However, she applied her magic to household chores and domestic relations. Samantha portrayed the tamed enchantress, subjugated by love of a man. Nevertheless, the mystery and danger of the sorcerer image were not entirely alien to her character.

The conflict between Samantha's desire to please her husband and her desire to use her considerable personal power was the basis of most of the <u>Bewitched</u> plots. Her resistance to male demands and domestic responsibility was like the imp's; however, it was not the tacit expression of disastrous incompetence, but rather a manifest exercise of her own power. Sometimes the basic conflict was represented as a clash between Endora and Darrin or between Samantha's family and his, but generally the theme was the same: Samantha could be a good woman (submissive, selfless) or a bad woman (powerful, willful, independent).

Another type that straddled the line between good woman-bad woman was the decoy. Like the witch, the decoy could charm and beguile; like the siren, she could seduce. What defined her as good was her allegiance to the team, her surrogate family. It was a male-oriented family, dominated by a fatherly leader and often consisting primarily of male agents. As the team's weakest member, she was tied to the imperatives of this male organization and thus ultimately controllable, despite all her charm and seduction.

Because of her obvious weakness the victim was also potentially controllable. Plus, she was usually a protagonist's sister, mother, wife, or lover and characterized as good for the sympathy inherent in that role. Nevertheless, there was in some victim stories an element of cheeky independence in her behavior prior to being assaulted, abused, or struck by disease. Indeed, her demise sometimes seemed retribution for her independence, particularly when it preceded her rejection of the series hero. Even the victim had her moments of willfulness, her "bad" behavior.

The composite impression of the good-bad images was a forceful endorsement of a secondary position for women, a place in the world as selfless, devoted adjuncts to men.   Any other female stance was, at best, an irritation, an interruption, and at worst, a threat to world order, a destructive force. Except in the rarest cases, expression of female autonomy, even expression of her own sexuality, was potentially harmful or dangerous.

Male characters were not presented in this way.   Although there were malevolent male characters who seemed to embody evil--gamblers, business barons, and mad scientists especially--they shared the set with an honorable, fallible hero and a herd of ordinary guys.   Typically, the hero was an ordinary human being who struggled with moral dilemmas while the primary female character offered him succor and support or embodied temptation and trouble.

The presentation of women always in relation to men, cheerleaders to the male players, is a male vision, the product of a medium in which male creators have predominated.   It is a vision that is part reality, part fantasy.

The reality of the images is evident in the recognizable similarities between the actions and events of the characters and the experiences of the viewers; the goodwife, harpy, and bitch display social behavior we encounter in society.   However, television has never been simply a reflection of society, as evident by the variety and abundance of content which grossly distorts the experience of its viewers. The distortion can be attributed to the aspect of television content that is fantasy.

Fantasy is an expression of myth, collective images of the culture, according to psychologist C. G. Jung.   In mythic images abstract woman is a good-bad dichotomy, a manifestation of the mother archetype, which is a particularly potent symbol in the unconscious of men.   Jung's descriptions of the archetype accommodate the character types described in this analysis: "The qualities associated with it are maternal solicitude and sympathy; the magic authority of the female, the wisdom and spiritual exaltation that transcend reason; [in addition to], anything secret, hidden, dark; anything that devours, seduces. "[1]

The good-bad typology of abstract woman has been found in media other than television, particularly literature, painting, and film.   If Jung's assumption is correct that the

mother archetype irrupts in the unconscious of men more
than women then we may expect to see more realistic, less
abstract female characters as women creators become more
numerous and influential in these media. Prime-time portrayals of the mid-eighties coinciding with increased numbers
of female writers in the television business promise just such
a trend. [2]

SOCIAL IMPLICATIONS OF FEMALE PORTRAYALS

Such media portrayals are not meaningless entertainment
but an index to what it means to be female in our society,
including the available options and the dimensions of the
role.   The types of characters women portray and the
stereotypes attributed to them convey beliefs and attitudes
about women and the kinds of behaviors women can be expected to enact.   The significance of these television characters and stories representing male and female figures in
recognizable situations is that they impact on the real world,
establishing expectations, validating preconceived notions,
and providing viewers with models of behavior for their own
lives.

There is a weighty body of evidence from social
science research that television's presentations influence
viewers.   Even the more specific issue of the effects of
television's image of women has been well-researched with
over 100 studies on television and sex roles published in
this country in the last fifteen years.   Although the results
of this research are not conclusive due to the difficulty of
isolating specific television effects from the other influences
of parents, peers, school, church, and so on, some reasonable inferences can be made about the medium's influence by
reviewing the findings of some of this research. [3]

One of the important, little-heralded findings of effects research is that viewers perceive television as representative of reality.   They use the medium as a source
of information about the world.   Among other data, television provides information about relationships and ways of
behaving, about women's place and potential in the world,
and about expectations of how they will act. [4]

Even more than formats designed to provide information, such as documentary and news, entertainment formats
impact on viewers because they foster learning that is indi-

rect and unintentional.   This incidental learning is effective
primarily because the messages are nonconscious and influence without the viewers' awareness.   Thus, TV characters
and situations assume an importance out of proportion to
their function as fantasy entertainment.   (Broadcasters, however, operate from a premise that reality and fantasy are
distinct.   Although they go to great trouble and expense to
create the illusion of reality, they are frequently surprised
at the degree to which television is taken seriously by the
viewer.   Most would agree with writer Jeff Greenfield who
protested recently: "There seems to be an unbroken premise that we can define reality by looking at what is on television; and that therefore the way to change reality is to
change what we see on television."   In fact, if the viewer
perceives television content as representative of reality, one
way to change society is to change what we see on television
[see J. Greenfield.   "TV Is Not the World."   Television
Quarterly, 1978, XV(3), 53].)

What is conveyed through television characters,
among other things, is information about roles, that is, social expectations for behavior.   There is strong social pressure for the individual to accept and internalize certain socially and culturally prescribed roles and not others, and to
endorse appropriate role behavior in others.   Maccoby and
Jacklin represented most socialization theorists in arguing
that appropriate role behavior is typically learned from ob-
serving the behavior of others, both real and mediated models.   Television affects the socialization process inadvertently by providing role models for its viewers in the fantasy
characters it represents as entertainment. [5]

There are a variety of roles present on television but
two kinds are of particular significance to a study of women
in the media: sex roles and occupational roles.   Sex roles
which relate to women by their definition are the most pervasive roles in society.   They apply to everyone in society
at any given moment (unlike roles such as doctor or custom-
er which are specific to the occasion) and they supersede and
affect other roles too.   Occupational roles are important for
the career options and employment norms they suggest to
viewers, for they define the expected behaviors for any oc-
cupant of a particular job or vocation.   In addition, television presents implied status associated with certain occupations, conveying higher status to those who give orders,
dress well, and spend freely.

Viewers learn sex role behavior and occupational roles from television. Furthermore, the medium also affects role expectation, the anticipation of how others will behave within the role framework. Viewers accept television models as realistic and anticipate others conforming to the expectations established by the medium.

The effects of learning roles from television are considerable, as judged by the importance of such socialization in affecting expectations of others' behavior and in shaping the viewers' own behavior. Role expectations affect perceptions of other people, members of certain occupations, for example, based upon the beliefs, attitudes, and behavior patterns associated with those occupations. Sex role expectation can result in the evaluation of one sex (male) as more socially desirable than the other, based upon the evaluation of sex-appropriate behaviors.

Learning roles from the media also affects viewers in their interpersonal relationships by establishing expectations for how others will act in these relationships. Exploration of such male-female interaction as intimacy, affection, control, and vulnerability on television conditions viewers to see certain patterns as "normal" in relationships. For children, the impact of media images is probably even more potent for they do not have much personal experience of past and present relationships on which to draw comparisons.

Another consequence of learning roles from the media may be negative evaluations of self, particularly if one learned a low status sex or occupational role. All three major theories of socialization (psychoanalytic, cognitive-developmental, and social learning theories) connect low self-esteem with the female sex role, and some psychologists attribute negative self images to occupational roles evaluated as low status. The projection of one's sex as foolish, helpless, and incompetent and/or one's occupation as unimportant and banal logically leads to feelings of inferiority when media images are viewed as representative. The more one believes what television portrays, the more dangerous are negative portrayals. Thus, the images and roles presented on fantasy formats have real life consequences, contributing to our expectations of others, to our own behaviors, and to self concepts.

TELEVISION PORTRAYALS: MEDIA MODELS FROM
HOUSEWIFE TO HOOKER

Episodic television's portrayals of women have not been a
fair and positive vision.   The implications of these video
images, especially for naive and frequent viewers, are provocative.   To the extent that television types are unrealistic,
the true images of women are ignored; to the extent that they
are negative, women are devalued.

Portrayals of female characters as a good-bad dichotomy are unrealistic representatives and therefore unproductive for both male and female viewers.   For men, the images of females promote unrealistic expectations about real
women who are neither exclusively good nor exclusively bad.
Male viewers with little direct experience in interpersonal
relationships with females (for example, adolescent boys),
could conclude that women are strange, unfriendly, asexual,
and dangerous to men.

There are few female character types with whom
male viewers could identify, thereby impressing on them
how strange and how different women are from them.   The
goodwife is a paragon, gently guiding the unsocialized males
in her life to correct behavior.   The imp is trouble for the
males around her.   The bitch and the harpy are independent
and strong-willed but obviously no friends to men.

In general, males and females are not friends, perhaps because of the unequal status between women and men
or a tendency to define male-female relations only in broad-
ly sexual terms.   Except in the courtesan and the decoy
shows, cross-gender interaction tends to be limited to marriage or rescue relationships.

Sweethearts and lovers are rare, too.   Sexual relationships are defined as power struggles in which the female
is either the victim or the male's downfall.   Typically, she's
an asexual being using her charms for personal profit.   The
sexual image of women--the harpy and the siren snaring innocent men or the decoy snaring guilty ones--undermines
healthy heterosexual relations.   Women's expressions of independence and sexual interest cannot always be threatening
to men and men are ill-served by media images that suggest
they are.

For women the good-bad typology presents a view of

self that is improbable or intolerable. Such images produce in women unreasonable expectations for their own behavior or negative self-images.   The choices between goody-goody goodwife and onerous harpy, between aging mum and spiteful bitch, between saloon belle and callous seducer are all specious.

"Bad" characters like the harpy, siren, and bitch, who are selfish and destructive, associate the female sex with emotionally-impoverished personalities, characters who have no empathy, no passion but for power over others.

Even the goodness of the goodwife has negative implications as a role model because its passive self-sacrifice omits the expression of self-interest and independence. This behavior is unhealthy, even dishonest, since the goodwife obviously has wants and needs but she expresses them only indirectly using subterfuge and manipulation to get her way. Her dishonesty disqualifies her as a fit model, particularly as a role model for wife, partner in a bond based on trust.

The imp and the witch are also bad models for married women. Imp characters are independent and honest as single women, but as wives they deceive and cajole. As for the witch, her charming guile is her trademark, perhaps a substitute for the overt power she denies herself.

For whatever reason, wives of past prime-time shows manipulated, duped, and deceived their husbands to get what they wanted.   The cost of this covert exercise of power was frequently loss of marital trust.   Both of the married relationships on I Love Lucy were characterized by deceit and chicanery, which to some extent was true of other marriages also.   Most of the husbands in prime-time comedies could be heard at some point in an episode to ask of their wives, "Is this some trick of yours?" Frequently it was a trick and the episode dealt with feminine deceit as the conflict. Perhaps the high incidence of manipulation and deceit among wives was a function of the lack of assertion by the females and the unequal distribution of economic and social powers to the males, but whatever the cause, television marriages were not characterized by trust.

Nor was wedlock characterized by expressions of intimacy.   Intimacy based on reciprocal dependence and attraction can be measured by such nonverbal cues as touching and by physical expressions of interdependency.   Few wives ex-

pressed both physical affection and psychological attachment.
Since intimacy is based on trust, this finding is not unex-
pected.   What it means is that viewers can't learn much
about closeness and mutual validation from the hundreds of
fictional marriages available in a decade of prime time.

The overall impression of the television wife as a
role model is a woman with a smile on her face and a trick
up her sleeve, who is submissive yet controlling.   She might
be a hostile bitch or a mischievous imp.   Most likely she is
a woman who is a secondary character in her own life, whose
conflicts, conversations, and concerns entirely revolve around
her husband.

As a model it is not unrealistic in that communication
researchers have found all these patterns of behavior in actual marriages.   The portrayal suffers, however, in failing
to depict the range of marital behaviors found among many
real-life couples.   Egalitarian marriages were invisible in
the first thirty years of prime time and wife-dominant marriages were never depicted, in spite of the reality of such
patterns among couples in the viewing audience.

Television's representative marriages weren't realistic and certainly weren't positive role models for female
viewers.   Submissive and manipulative behavior is no tool
for intimate relationships, nor is deceit amusing in real life.
Moreover, the model was deficient in other ways, particularly in the presentation of a married adult as asexual.   Sex
was intimated on the courtesan, siren, and harpy shows and
by the mid-seventies the subject was discussed and dissected
on a weekly basis on some show or other, but adult sexual
love was invisible and wives were still portrayed without
sexual appeal or sexual appetites until the Hart to Hart show
of the 1980's.

This flawed rendition of the role of wife is the most
common picture of the female sex we have had for decades.
Less common, though more positive, are the portraits of
unmarried women, especially the imp, the courtesan, and
the matriarch.   These models are flawed, too: the imp's
independence is viewed as disturbing; the courtesan's single
state is reluctant and somewhat tainted; and the matriarch
derives her power from her dead husband or her children.
Nevertheless, they have much to recommend them; they are
adventurous and spirited and they depict women of some
self-worth.   The validity and merit of these models contrast

with the damaging proscription implies by many of the other
female images.

Perhaps the most pernicious image is that of victim
because it has been identified primarily with female characters.   The prevalence of portraying the victim as female
fosters the association of victims with women, thereby projecting a helpless, abused image of women.   The effect on
the minds of female viewers is indoctrination into what
Brownmiller has labeled "victim mentality."[6]   Identification
with female characters who become victimized leads females
in our society to believe that women are helpless figures in
a threatening world.   Regardless of the nature of the attack,
passivity and appeal for male rescue are seen as the victim's
only defenses.

The decoy presented a similar set of conclusions for
female viewers, for although the decoy possesses some heroic traits, she is vulnerable and needs male deliverance in
most escapades.   She is a sort of professional victim, a
stand-in for less capable female subjects.   The inference in
both cases is that females are defenseless creatures, liable
to misfortune and abuse.

For males there were several figures with whom to
identify and those who rejected the guilt of the aggressor
could choose the image of the knight, the rescuer.   For females, however, there were far too few adventurers and
bold figures to counter the effect of the myriad of passive
victims and vulnerable decoys in dire need of male protec-
tion.   The television woman had a severely limited role and
as she aged, the road narrowed.

Mirroring the images of females, their occupational
roles were constrictive as well.   Prominent male characters
depicted doctors, detectives, astronauts, engineers, writers,
ranchers, riveters, farmers, mechanics, policemen, lawyers, and spies.   Women were seldom shown employed but
those who did enact occupational roles were confined to a
narrow range of options.   On a typical night the female occupational roles which aired were those of housewife, receptionist, and whore.   It is an unbalanced selection of choices
from which to mold a life.

The role of housewife, a married female character
who worked without salary inside the home, was ubiquitous
on television until quite recently.   In the first thirty years

of prime time the housewife was seen in comic and dramatic format, in nineteenth-century ranch house and modern-day apartment, in poverty and in wealth.

Although the housewife functions were viewed as indispensable in several series, the role appeared to be one for which criteria other than sex were irrelevant and unnecessary. Housework as depicted on television programs was trivial and required little skill or talent to perform. Tasks involved cosmetic chores such as dusting or setting tables, the absence of which would scarcely be missed in the average home. Other aspects of the housewife role, including scrubbing, laundering, baking, and dishwashing, were invisible. Only the imp characters performed these tasks and then it was cause for fun, the result being a fifty-foot cake or a chair upholstered in paint and feathers.

Witch characters present another fun way to be a housewife. The witch is not a domestic creature by nature any more than the imp is, but whereas the imp wishes for magic formulas, the witch actually employs them. When the imp enters the kitchen, batter spatters on walls and floors; when the witch produces a cake, no batter ever appears. Both impressions belie the real drudgery of step-by-step procedures and care and the daily monotony of cooking and cleaning.

The television picture portrays neither the drudgery nor the accomplishments of the housewife experience. Character housewives are not shown washing floors and windows and scrubbing bathrooms, nor are they depicted doing the highly skilled work associated with the role. Entertainment housewives aren't seen sewing a needlepoint or baking a soufflé, skilled tasks for which they are celebrated in other formats and in other media. (Housewives in episodic formats present a marked contrast to the role models evident in commercials. During the commercial breaks, the viewer sees housewives who are obsessed with their role, worrying about how fresh their houses smell and how clean their husbands' shirt collars and their children's jeans look. Successful household maintenance is serious business on soap and wax commercials and the inherent skills of the role are highly appreciated on ads for vitamin supplements. When the entertainment format resumes, however, the viewer sees the importance of the housewife recede as the problems of other family members become focal.)

The only other identifying characteristic of character housewives besides their sex and ability to do light housework is that they are married. Not only are housewives by definition married women, but married women characters are overwhelmingly identified as housewives. Single women on episodic shows are sometimes employed but with few exceptions married women are housewives irrespective of format. On some shows, the housewife character is depicted as a former career woman who discontinued employment after marriage, choosing the immaterial rewards of domestic service over other occupations.

Other than housewives there are the women characters who perform domestic duties, caring for and feeding a household of people who are not their own families. There are the boarding-house keepers, maids, housekeepers, and governesses who generally perform the housewife's chores with the difference that they get paid for their trouble. Among the surveyed comic characters, paid domestic work was the most common occupation after housewife.

Occupational role models other than housewife are not well-represented on network programming. Research in 1974 found that major female characters are three times more likely to portray housewives than any other occupational roles. In the decade preceding, the ratio was more skewed: 5 to 1. Those characters who were the exception portrayed receptionists, nurses, cops, waitresses, writers, entertainers, and whores. Not only were males depicted in a greater variety of roles but they were far more numerous in those roles in which role models of both sexes appeared. For example, the ratio of male to female doctors in popular programs was 20 to 1. The most popular occupation for males was police officer and there the males outnumbered females 25 to 1. Depicting a lone female among many males was popular, encouraging a picture of a career woman as unique in the world of working men. Mary Richards of The Mary Tyler Moore Show and Elaine Nardo of Taxi are two of the most recent in a long list of lone women in the workplace . [7]

Males and females occupy different status positions in occupational roles, too. Typical is Eve Whitfield of Ironside, a policewoman who worked with a law student, a police sergeant, and the former chief of police. Almost without exception, males embodied higher status occupations than females where differences existed; Big Town, Perry Mason,

M*A*S*H, and Alice illustrate the trend. Other evidence of
the inferior status of female models is the pattern of depicting males in controlling occupations and females in service
occupations. (Television audiences have been able to see
even the poor and desperate male characters own their own
businesses since the 1952 debut of Life with Luigi and continuing the tradition on Happy Days, Chico and the Man, Sanford
and Son, Laverne and Shirley, and Archie's Place.) Thus
male lawyers judged and males in business owned the store,
whereas females in business and law portrayed secretaries,
clerks, receptionists, and switchboard operators. The relationships between the sexes were necessarily ones of unequal
partners, since one took orders from the other. The attitude
of deference some females adopted toward their male bosses
further reflected the female's lower status.

The pattern is repeated in hospitals of the airwaves.
Nurses, nurses aides, and other female hospital personnel
resemble clerical females in that their work is service work
and their status is secondary. Their occupational activities
include making beds, serving food, and ministering to the
needs of the sick. Their relationships with male personnel
are typified by order-taking and obedience.

In general, the television rendition of the working
woman's role is a copy of its portrayal of the housewife.
Although the clerk, nurse, or waitress be mentally, moral-
ly, and constitutionally superior, she is dependent on a male
for supervision and direction, in the way the housewife is
economically and socially dependent upon her husband. The
female wage earner further mirrors the domestic model in
the activities she performs: nurses clean rooms, arrange
flowers, dress, and coddle their charges as if they were
children; receptionists make coffee and attend to their bosses;
and waitresses serve food. Thus was the appearance of the
woman's domestic relationships duplicated in other contexts.

Both comic and dramatic programming consistently
project a picture of unemployed, married women and salaried, single women. The dichotomy of homemaker-wage
earner segregates the two primary arenas of relegating the
home to the housewife and leaving the workplace a single's
domain. The importance of being single is further illus-
trated by the numerous occupational role models whose primary qualification seems to be sexual attractiveness. Decoy cops, skirted spies, and undercover agents depict sa-
lacious seducers of men whose job descriptions were designed

as distraction. Some in this party of sirens appear to be little more than salaried hookers, discipline and monthly pay distinguishing them from television whores.

In the prostitute category there are examples enough. Seven percent of the regular characters and nearly 20 percent of the guest characters on dramatic shows occupy positions that could be variously described as chippy (saloon keeper, dance hall girl, call girl, whore, madam, moll). Their role consists of pleasing men, the physical manifestations of which were only suggested on network programming. The effect of these portrayals on young female viewers seeking role models cannot be assessed but the positive impression of their appealing self-sufficiency cannot be denied.

The other role models of note are crooks, con artists, and witches. The first two categories are negative models. The witch, if it can be considered a role, is one, like a queen, to which one must be born. The dominant options for female choice reduce to two kinds of women-- homemakers or hookers. Television homemakers (nursemaids, office-wives) were found to be benign but banal. Hookers (decoy agents, show girls) in their jeweled and satin finery were symbols of impulsiveness and independence. The latter type was young, single, sexy and the former was sexually immobile, frumpy, and married.

These representations were not reflective of the real world. Throughout the thirty-year period, most working women were married, yet television did not reflect this situation. Prime time presented female characters as either working or married, effectively representing the two roles as mutually exclusive. The dichotomy of homemaker-wage earner suggests two primary arenas, relegating the home to the housewife and leaving the workplace a single's domain. Emotional and sympathetic behavior is prescribed for the housewife role and emotionally sterile, yet dominant and self-reliant behavior for the occupational role. The ambivalence and conflict perpetuated by the simultaneous performance of both roles--a circumstance faced by most employed women--was not addressed in prime-time formats.

Furthermore the medium probably contributes to the conflict experienced by employed wives by the tacit endorsement of the housewife role as feminine and good. Domesticity is "feminine"--nurturant, sympathetic, passive--and it

is associated with good characters: Harriet Nelson, Laura
Petrie, Victoria Barkley, and others.   On the other hand,
the female's pursuit of career goals is perceived as a threat
to the conventional relations between the sexes, as evident
in the imp, harpy, and courtesan epilogues.   The conclusion
to be drawn from such presentations is that the housewife
role is the only appropriate choice for women to make.   Not
only did the medium miss an opportunity to present role
models for married working women, it denigrated their pursuit of gainful employment.

PUTTING THE CHARACTERS IN CONTEXT

Character portrayals and epilogues which have negative implications for viewers are obviously not intentional misrep-
resentations.   They are not the result of a conspiracy against
working wives, powerful mothers, seductive females, or any
other women.   They are unintentional products of fantasy,
cultural clichés triggered by ideas and feelings which arise
in response to everyday experiences.   They can be best un-
derstood within the context of the times in which they arise.

        Although the themes and perspectives have most often
been traditionally masculine, their success with huge seg-
ments of our society testifies that they have served female
fantasy as well.   The most popular character types and
themes have appealed to both sexes, sometimes for different reasons.   The everyday experiences of each decade seem
to have fostered types and motifs tailored for the times.
Thus, the rise and wane in popularity of certain themes,
characters, and types of programs make sense against a
backdrop of actual events of the time.

        The economic and social conditions of the 1950's
created an atmosphere of nostalgia for previous times, a
nostalgia reflected in the television content Americans chose.
During a period characterized by recession, inflation, and
fierce job competition, prime time's popular situation comedies portrayed families in circumstances of affluence and
fathers in constant leisure.   In a decade of cold war aggression and communist threat, prime time Westerns depicted clear-cut enemies and the moral superiority of the
hero.   Prime time also reflected change and anxiety about
woman's place in society in its depiction of the decade's
popular character types: the goodwife, the courtesan, and
the imp.

The image of the domestic goodwife was an argument in support of homemaking as a means of personal fulfillment and marital satisfaction. The goodwife was a visible success in her role, a model of adaptability. The image was a collective yearning for other times when the family was a woman's central concern and the job market belonged to men.

Back to back the goodwife shows said that the woman's place was in the home and the Western agreed that it most especially was not on the frontier. The frontier was a male preserve where women were an intrusion, a disturbance; those unfortunate females who ventured on the scene were eliminated or forced to flee. The exception was the courtesan, a survivor and a man-pleaser by trade. The courtesan was an entrepreneur, distinguished from domestic pleasers of men as much by her unmarried independence as by painted face and peacock feathers. She was comfortable in a man's world but in no way a contender for the manly tasks of gun-slinging, cow-punching, or peace-keeping.

To male viewers the courtesan was a reassurance that some women weren't after their jobs or a threat to their freedom. To women viewers she was the veiled voice of resistance. Her impudent lifestyle and freedom from domination and domesticity were a fantasy of sedition for working wives, many of whom served two masters. Her audacious accouterments were an affirmation of feminity in a male world. The courtesan was an image both sexes could enjoy in equal measure.

The image of the female imp, which was also prevalent during the 1950's, was an expression of dissatisfaction with domesticity for female audience members. Characters like Lucy Ricardo articulated women's dissatisfaction with the limitations and restrictions their domestic role imposed on them. Women audience members could identify with Lucy's dreams of stardom and the imp's casual neglect of domestic duties.

At the same time, imp shows offered justification for the imposition of domesticity on women because the stories clearly demonstrated that females were incapable by temperament or talent to compete in the job market. For men who could identify with the husband characters, the shows offered expression of the frustrations of living with wives who were not fulfilled by domesticity but who were unsuited for anything else. By the same token, imp

shows offered both men and women an opportunity to laugh
at a character in a worse state than they; a character at
continual odds with authority figures; a character bedeviled
by schedules, chores, responsibilities, restricted by society's rules but unable to break them.   Like Chaplin's hobo,
the imp's predominant appeal may have been as a symbol of
the anxiety and frustration of the powerless.

Situation comedies of the 1960's also offered expression for the anxiety and frustration of its audience members.
The 1960 comedy images of superwomen provided opportunity
for the expression of discontent for women as well as men.
For women audience members, the superhuman capabilities
of the witches and genies on situation comedies were a reflection of both fantasy and frustration.   Demands made on
women's energies and abilities increased in the 1960's as
more and more women, especially married women, entered
the work force.   Thus, they were expected to meet the demands of a job or career and simultaneously care for home
and family.   The appeal of a character like Samantha Stevens, who could produce meals with a twitch of her nose,
should not have been surprising.

For male audience members, the bevy of faithful
fantasy women evident during a decade of increased feminist protest was a fantasy of a world of capable, non-
competitive women who catered to male needs and desires.
The superhuman characters who appeared on the television
screen, although possessed of unordinary capabilities, were
nonetheless dominated by the men they served.   Thus, the
image may have represented a nostalgia for both sexes--a
nostalgia for a time of clear-cut sex role prescriptions, of
dominant men and dependent women who had separate spheres
of influence.

In dramatic content of the decade, decoy shows dealt
with some of the same anxieties in the presentation of the
female agent whose seductive distraction complemented the
male heroes' intelligence and strength.   The message to
both sexes was an endorsement of women's role as sex object rather than combatant in the struggle for justice.   As
a sex object, the decoy in no way threatened the authority
of the male heroes; her sexuality and vulnerability confined
her to one role only and that was clearly a supportive role.
The decoy series was an echo of radical Stokely Carmichael's
retort that the position of women in social reform was
"prone. "

The decoy served as a fantasy figure for women, too, for she bridged the world of daring adventure appropriate to males and the glittery world of fashion and ornament associated with females. At a time when women were increasingly participating in the workforce and female workers were lobbying to enter all-male preserves of the boardroom, the courtroom, the coal mine, even the vicarage, the decoy's presence among men was a projection that a woman could succeed in the male world without endangering her credentials in the female one. At the same time, her affectionate, asexual relations with her co-workers reassured the wives of male workers that seductive working women were only a threat to the enemy.

By the 1960's, the decoy had become an avenging angel. Although she was vulnerable to attack and capture, she was not without resources. Not the least of which was the support of the crime-fighting unit to which she belonged. She was a victim who was capable of avenging injustice and oppression, her victories particularly appealing to the middle class of both sexes. At a time of political betrayals and undeclared wars, of social revolutions, and changes in mores and morals, the decoy was an extension of the anger, frustration, and resentment of the middle class. She infiltrated organizations, youth groups, and subcultures which threatened to subvert the status quo and she disrupted or destroyed them. On Mission Impossible and other spy series, the decoy worked to destabilize governments, defuse rebellions and undermine governments and political leaders opposed to the United States or its allies. On Mod Squad, Ironside, and Policewoman, the decoy infiltrated the youth culture, the inner-city poor, and political reformist bands, giving voice to the anger of the newly christened "silent majority," who were troubled and outraged by the dissent of these groups.

The demands of women's political groups were equally enraging to the middle class majority but this group was not depicted on decoy programs, perhaps because the decoy too closely resembled the dissidents in circumstance and outlook. Instead, backlash from the woman's movement was intimated in other genres, particularly in the rash of violent, male-only crime series whose very names expressed machismo: Baretta, Bronk, Cannon, Kojak, Shaft, Starsky and Hutch. (Many of the names recall objects which symbolize male sexual organs [column, cannon, shaft], an association which was further suggested in some series by

favored objects of the hero, such as Bronk's pipe and Kojak's lollypops. Such associations between the hero and
some penis-type object have long been represented in action
formats. In several series the object was a gun: Colt .45,
Yancy Derringer, Restless Gun, The Rifleman, Wanted:
Dead or Alive, Magnum, P. I. Other phallic weapons were
the hero's special trademark in Bat Masterson, The Adventures of Jim Bowie, and Zorro. The theme of sexual po-
tency underscored in these series was embellished by the
fact that regardless of the situation, the hero's weapon never
failed him.) Masculine dominance was implicit in these
crime dramas' all-male environs. It was made explicit in
these shows by the depiction of violent victimization, invariably an act of aggression committed by a male or a gang of
males against a female.

    The woman who trespassed in these male environs
was one of two types: a bitch--a debilitating virus in society; or a victim--a scapegoat for all hostility against women.
The masculine habitat of Baretta or Kojak expressed a nostalgia for lost adolescence but the high incidence of the two
female types in otherwise womanless worlds suggests an unspoken misogynist resentment as notable as the male cama-
raderie underlying the drama. The concurrent media attention given on news and documentary programs to the demand
of women for access into male-dominated arenas of the marketplace could not have been unrelated to the hostility expressed in machismo drama.

    The reasons that women watched the violent victimi-
zation of their sex were less obvious. Perhaps they identified with the victim, relating to the powerless position which
she projected. If the backlash and antagonism toward wom-
en expressed in the dramas surfaced in their own lives, female viewers surely related to a defenseless character in a
hostile world. Irrespective of their personal circumstances,
they could probably relate to the rescue theme inherent in
the victim's dependent relationship with the hero, for it not
only duplicated the father-daughter bond of childhood but it
reiterated a cultural legend from childhood--Sleeping Beauty.

    Shows such as Rhoda, The Bob Newhart Show, and
Three's Company served to reassure their audiences that
women in the pursuit of economic and social gains could
still be feminine, relating to men in submissive ways. A
counterpoint to these "liberated"-yet-tame female figures
was the harpy, who testified that women in some quarters

were becoming more militant. If the harpy failed to find
romantic bliss, her career success was a plus, an indication of the ambivalence Americans were feeling about assertive women in the bedroom and boardroom. For both
sexes the popular comedies expressed the frustration and
difficulties of coping with changing norms, mores, expectations, and aspirations.

        In the most popular show of the 1970's, <u>All in the
Family</u>, the concept of coping with change was preeminent.
This situation comedy opened the show every week with the
theme song, "Those Were the Days." Archie Bunker,
struggling to cope with contemporary problems and issues
with an outdated value system based on WASP male suprem-
acy, expressed nostalgia for the days when "girls were girls
and men were men." For male audience members, their
own anxiety at relating to wives, daughters, and female co-
workers demanding autonomy and recognition found expression in Archie's abrasive anger or son-in-law Michael's
frustrated bewilderment.

        <u>All in the Family</u> appealed to females, too, especially
in the characters of Edith Bunker and her daughter, Gloria.
Like Archie, Edith expressed nostalgia for the "old days"
and served to reassure family-centered women that the old
values were still important. Edith demonstrated that such
values could be compatible with ideas of liberation which
were introduced by characters Gloria and Irene. The fond-
ness and emotional support these three characters offered
for each other attested to the compatibility of traditional and
non-traditional women. In this, too, the comedy supported
traditional values while expressing the conflict and confusion
experienced by the average person confronting social change.

        Television's patterns have occurred in cycles. After
a decade of womanless series came the decoys, the superhuman types, and the matriarchs. After a string of single
father comedies in the late sixties came the strong-soft female leads of <u>Bionic Woman, Amy Prentiss, The Ghost and
Mrs. Muir</u>, and <u>The Mary Tyler Moore Show</u>. By the late
seventies those female heroes had departed and machismo
drama and clown comedy were usurping the ratings. Bob
Schiller of <u>All in the Family</u> noted the void in 1978:
"Maude's gone. Mary's gone. There's no character like
that on the air."[8]

        Another cycle is already beginning. In the 1980's

there are wonderful, warm exceptions to the general picture
on prime time.   Most of these wonderful figures are legacies
of the MTM production company, which originated The Mary
Tyler Moore Show of the 1970's.   There is Elaine Nardo,
Taxi's single, working mother who was invented by three co-
creators of The Mary Tyler Moore Show: Jim Brooks, Stan
Daniels, and Ed. Weinberger.   Other MTM alumni created
Joyce Davenport, Hill Street Blues' sassy, sexy lawyer;
Laura Holt, who heads her own detective agency on Reming-
ton Steele; Diane Chambers, the waitress with a master's
degree who works on Cheers; St. Elsewhere's Dr. Annie
Cavanero; and architect Elyse Keaton (played by Meredith
Baxter Birney) of Family Ties.   This last character is one
of the most fully-developed female characters of the lot, a
warm, sexual wife-mother with a sense of humor about herself and her life.   Some of these characters did not live much
more than a season but they brightened the picture while
they lived and hinted at new trends in the images of women.

It's certainly time.   Twenty years have passed since
Betty Friedan published The Feminine Mystique, documenting
the dissatisfaction American women felt with domesticity.
American viewers have spent over three decades watching
male heroes and their adventures, muddied visions of boy-
hood adolescence replete with illusions of women as witches,
bitches, mothers, and imps.   Television has ignored the
most important part of women's lives--their concepts, sensations, aspirations, desires, and dreams.   It's time to tell
the stories of female heroes--heading families, heading cor-
porations, conquering fears, and coping with change.   Good
models are needed to connect women to each other and to
their society.

CHAPTER 1

1. Inkeles, A. "Society, social structure and child socialization," in J. A. Clausen (ed.), Socialization
   and Society. Boston: Little, Brown, 1968, p. 121.

2. Three sources discuss studies relevant to imitation of
   media models: Bandura, A., and R. H. Walters,
   Social learning and personality development. New
   York: Holt, Rinehart & Winston, 1963; Hyman, H. H.,
   "Mass communications and socialization," in W. P.
   Davidson and F. T. C. Yu (eds.), Mass communica-
   tion research: Major issues and future directions.
   New York: Praeger, 1974; and J. M. McLeod and
   G. J. O'Keefe, "The socialization perspective and
   communication," in F. G. Kline and P. J. Tichenor
   (eds.), Current perspectives in mass communication
   research. Belmont, Calif.: Sage, 1972.

3. Maccoby, E., and C. Jacklin, The psychology of sex
   differences. Stanford, Calif.: Stanford University
   Press, 1974.

4. Comments on source material for Star Wars and Raiders of the Lost Ark are by S. Spielberg in a personal
   interview, Los Angeles, California, in August 1981.
      Television's source material has been analyzed by
   Muriel G. Cantor in Prime-Time Television: Content
   and Control. Beverly Hills, Calif.: Sage, 1980; and
   by Horace Newcomb, "Towards a Television Aesthetic,"
   in Newcomb (ed.), The Critical View: Television.
   New York: Oxford, 1976, pp. 273-289.

CHAPTER 2

1. See Bob Shanks' The Cool Fire: How to Make It in
    Television (New York: Vintage, 1977) and Dick
    Levinson and Bill Links' insightful book, Stay Tuned:
    An Inside Look at the Making of Prime Time Televi-
    sion (New York: St. Martin's Press, 1981) for two
    views of the business of attracting audiences.

2. A. Schneider, ABC Vice-President of Program Prac-
    tices, quoted in Bob Alley's Television: Ethics for
    Hire? (Nashville, Tenn.: Abingdon, 1977), p. 36.

3. Levinson and Link, op. cit., p. 30.

4. Interview with R. Carroll, Burbank, California, on
    August 8, 1978.

5. Interview with R. Weiskopf, Los Angeles, California,
    August 1978.

6. Carroll, loc. cit.

7. E. Hammer, quoted in Alley, op. cit., p. 120.

8. Shanks, op. cit., p. 305.

9. Levinson and Link, op. cit., p. 31.

10. Ibid., p. 30.

11. Courtney, A. Cited in Panorama, 1(2), March 1980,
     p. 23.

12. Interview w. P. Jones and D. Reiker, Hollywood,
     California, on February 9, 1982.

13. Levinson and Link, op. cit., p. 97.

14. I. Lupino. Cited in M. Rosen's Popcorn Venus:
     Women, Movies and the American Dream. (New
     York: Avon, 1973), p. 403.

15. Jones and Reiker, op. cit.

16. N. Lear, quoted in Alley, op. cit., inside flap.

17. Levinson and Link, op. cit., p. 105.

18. Norman Lear, cited in Alley, op. cit., p. 132.

19. Alan Alda, cited in Alley, op. cit., p. 33.

20. Information based on interviews with writers from 1978 to 1982.

21. Jim Brooks, cited in Alley, op. cit., p. 30.

22. Fay Kanin, cited in Bill Froug's The Screenwriter Looks at Screenwriting. (New York: Dell, 1972), p. 128.

23. Information based on interviews with writers from 1978 to 1982.

24. Ibid.

25. Interview with M. Davis and B. Carroll, Burbank, California, on August 8, 1978.

CHAPTER 3

1. I Love Lucy; "The great train robbery"; Viacom No. 1050-132; 1955.

2. Ibid.

3. Beverly Hillbillies; 1966.

4. Beverly Hillbillies; 1962.

5. Bonanza; "Little Joe and Calamity Jane"; 1968.

6. Laverne and Shirley; "Lamplighters"; (date unknown).

7. Laverne and Shirley; 1977.

8. Laverne and Shirley; "Lamplighters."

CHAPTER 4

1. The Adventures of Ozzie and Harriet; "Volunteer fireman"; Episode No. 27-129; 1957.

2. The Adventures of Ozzie and Harriet; "David's engage-ment"; Episode No. 27-114; 1957.

3. Dragnet; 1955.

4. Big Town; "Reservoir story"; 1955.

5. The Dick Van Dyke Show; "The necklace"; 1961.

6. The Dick Van Dyke Show; "New act in town"; 1965.

7. All in the Family; "Second honeymoon"; Episode No. 0412; 1973.

CHAPTER 5

1. The Mary Tyler Moore Show; "What are friends for?"; 1974.

2. The Mary Tyler Moore Show; "Anybody who hates kids and dogs"; 1974.

3. The Mary Tyler Moore Show; 1975.

4. Ibid.

5. M*A*S*H; "Your hit parade"; 1977.

6. M*A*S*H; "Under fire"; 1975.

7. M*A*S*H; "The MASH olympics"; 1977.

8. M*A*S*H; 1975.

9. M*A*S*H; "Col. Potter takes over"; 1975.

10. M*A*S*H; "Under fire"; 1975.

11. The Dick Van Dyke Show; "New act in town"; 1965.

12. The Mary Tyler Moore Show; 1974.

CHAPTER 6

1. Dragnet; 1955.

2. <u>Ironside</u>; "Programmed for danger"; 1968.

3. <u>Medical Center</u>; "The betrayal"; (date unknown).

4. Ibid.

5. <u>Streets of San Francisco</u>; "The victims"; 1973.

6. Ibid.

7. <u>Maude</u>; "The new housekeeper"; 1974.

8. Ibid.

9. <u>Maude</u>; "The kiss"; 1974.

10. <u>Maude</u>; "Vivian's party"; 1974.

11. <u>Maude</u>; "The cabin"; 1974.

CHAPTER 7

1. Turow, J., "Advising and ordering; daytime, prime time," <u>Journal of Communication</u>, 24(2), 1974, pp. 138-141. Head, S. W., "Content analysis of television dramatic programs," <u>Quarterly of Film, Radio and Television</u>, 9, 1954, pp. 175-194. Greenberg, B. S.; Simmons, K. W.; Hogan, L.; and Adkin, C. K., "The demography of fictional TV characters," in B. S. Greenberg (ed.), <u>Life on television: content analysis of U.S. TV drama</u>. Norwood, N.J.: Ablex, 1980.

2. <u>Streets of San Francisco</u>; "The victims"; 1973.

3. <u>Big Valley</u>; "Teacher of outlaws"; 1968.

4. <u>Big Valley</u>; "Presumed dead"; 1968.

5. <u>Medical Center</u>; "The judgement"; (date unknown).

6. <u>Marcus Welby, M.D.</u>; "Kiley in love"; 1974.

CHAPTER 8

1. <u>Ironside</u>; "Programmed for danger; 1969.

1. Charlie's Angels; "Angel in a box"; 1979.

3. Hart to Hart; 1979.

4. Hart to Hart; 1979.

5. Ibid.

CHAPTER 9

1. Maverick; "Point blank"; 1958.

2. Big Valley; "By fires unseen"; (date unknown).

CHAPTER 10

1. Gunsmoke; "Kimbro"; 1972.

2. Maverick; "According to Hoyle"; 1958.

3. Ibid.

4. Ibid.

5. Alice; 1979.

6. Ibid.

7. Gunsmoke; 1966.

8. Alice; "Florence of Arabia"; 1978.

CHAPTER 11

1. Ellman, M., Thinking about women. New York: Harcourt, Brace, Jovanovich, 1968. Dworkin, A., Woman hating. New York: Dutton, 1974. Williams,
S. R., Riding the nightmare: Women and witchcraft.
New York: Atheneum, 1978.

2. Bewitched; "Man or a mouse"; 1967.

3. Ibid.

4. Ibid.

5. <u>I Dream of Jeannie</u>; "I wish I were in Paris"; 1966.

CHAPTER 12

1. <u>Maverick</u>; 1958.

2. <u>Big Valley</u>; "Teacher of outlaws"; 1968.

3. <u>Big Valley</u>; "Presumed dead"; 1968.

4. <u>Big Valley</u>; "Teacher of outlaws"; 1968.

5. <u>Big Valley</u>; "Fall of a hero"; 1968.

6. <u>Big Valley</u>; "Teacher of outlaws"; 1968.

7. <u>Big Valley</u>; "Presumed dead"; 1968.

8. <u>Big Valley</u>; "Teacher of outlaws"; 1968.

9. <u>Big Valley</u>; "Presumed dead"; 1968.

10. <u>Big Valley</u>; "By fires unseen"; 1967.   <u>Big Valley</u>;
    "Fall of a hero"; 1968.

11. <u>Big Valley</u>; "By fires unseen"; 1967.

12. <u>Big Valley</u>; "Presumed dead"; 1968.

13. <u>Bonanza</u>; "Nice, friendly little town"; 1969.

14. <u>Charlie's Angels</u>; "Angels on vacation"; 1978.

CHAPTER 13

1. Jung, C. G., <u>The archetypes and the collective un-
    conscious.</u> New York: Bollinger, 1959, p. 82.

2. Discussion of good-bad imagery in other media is
    found in L. M. Brown, "Sexism in Western Art,"
    in J. Freeman (ed.), Women: a feminist perspec-
    <u>tive</u>. Palo Alto, Calif.: Mayfield, 1975; L. Field-

ler, Love and death in the American novel. New
York: Stein and Day, 1975; M. A. Ferguson,
Images of women in literature. Boston: Houghton
Mifflin, 1977; and M. Haskell, From reverence to
rape: the treatment of women in the movies. New
York: Holt, Rinehart and Winston, 1974.

3. See L. J. Busby, "Sex-role research on the mass
media," Journal of Communication, 25(4), 1975, pp.
107-131; R. M. Liebert, J. M. Neale, and E. S.
Davidson, The early window: effects of television on
children and youth. New York: Pergamon Press,
1973; R. W. Poulos, E. A. Rubinstein, and R. M.
Liebert, "Positive social learning," Journal of Communication, 25(4), 1975, pp. 90-97.

4. Perceptions of television are the subject of two recent
research pieces: G. A. Comstock and G. Lindsay,
Television and human behavior: the research horizon,
future and present. Santa Monica, Calif.: Rand,
1975; and B. S. Greenberg and B. Reeves, "Children
and the perceived reality of television," Journal of
Social Issues, 32(4), 1976, pp. 80-97.

5. Incidental learning from television has been the subject
of numerous behavioral research studies. A discussion of recent research on television's effect on children is found in Gerald Lesser's book, Children and
television: lessons from Sesame Street. New York:
Random House, 1975. Adult learning is evaluated in
a paper by S. Ward and M. L. Ray, "Cognitive responses to mass communication: results from laboratory studies and a field experiment." Paper prepared for the Association for Education in Journalism
Convention in San Diego, 1974. Two sources discuss studies relevant to imitation of media models:
A. Bandura and R. H. Walters, Social learning and
personality development. New York: Holt, Rinehart
& Winston, 1963; see also, E. Maccoby and C. Jacklin, The psychology of sex differences. Stanford,
Calif.: Stanford University Press, 1974.

6. Brownmiller, S. Against our will: men, women and
rape. New York: Simon & Schuster, 1975.

7. Research findings refer to the present study, completed in 1980. For another recent study of occupa-

tional roles on television, see B. S. Greenberg, et al., "The demography of fictional TV characters," in Greenberg (ed.), <u>Life on television: content analyses of U.S. TV drama.</u> Norwood, N.J.: Ablex, 1980.

8. Interview with Bob Schiller and Bob Weiskopf, August 17, 1978, in Hollywood, California.

★ BIBLIOGRAPHY

Alley, B. Television: ethics for hire? Nashville, Tenn.: Abingdon, 1977, p. 36.

Anderson, R. E., and E. Jolley. "Stereotyped traits and sex roles in humorous drawings," Communication Research, 4(4), 1977, pp. 453-484.

Arens, W., and S. P. Montague. The American dimension: cultural myths and social realities. New York: Alfred, 1976.

Arlen, M. J. "The media dramas of Norman Lear," in H. Newcomb (ed.), Television: the critical view. New York: Oxford, 1976.

Bandura, A. "Social learning theory of identification processes," in D. Goslin (ed.), Handbook of socialization theory and research. Chicago: Rand McNally, 1969.

_____, and R. H. Walters. Social learning and personality development. New York: Holt, Rinehart & Winston, 1963.

Bellman, B. L., and B. Jules-Rosette. A paradigm for looking: crosscultural research with visual media. Norwood, N.J.: Ablex, 1977.

Bennett, R. M. "Who should control television?" Television Quarterly, XV(2), 1978, pp. 73-77.

Bernard, J. The future of marriage. New York: Macmillan, 1971.

Beuf, A. "Doctor, lawyer, household drudge," Journal of Communication, 24(2), 1974, pp. 142-145.

Blake, R. A. "O Maude, poor Maude," in F. H. Voelker and L. A. Voelker (eds.), Mass media: forces in our society. New York: Harcourt Brace, 1975.

Boyle, C. D., and B. J. Wahlstrom. "Cultural analysis: unmasking the makings of oppression," The University of Michigan Papers in Women's Studies, (1), 1974, pp. 10-43.

Brim, O. G. "Adult socialization," in J. A. Clausen (ed.), Socialization and Society. Boston: Little, Brown, 1968.

Brown, L. Television: the business behind the box. New York: Harcourt Brace Jovanovich, 1971.

Brownmiller, S. Against our will: men, women and rape. New York: Simon and Schuster, 1975.

Busby, L. J. "Defining the sex role standard in commercial network television programs directed toward children," Journalism Quarterly, 51(4), 1974, pp. 690-696.

_____. "Sex role research on the mass media," Journal of Communication, 25(4), 1974, pp. 107-131.

Cantor, M. G. "Comparison of tasks and roles of males and females in commercials aired by WRC-TV during composite week," Women in the wasteland fight back: a report on the image of women portrayed in TV programming. Washington, D.C.: National Organization for Women, 1972.

_____. Prime-time television: content and control. Beverly Hills, Calif.: Sage, 1980.

_____. The Hollywood producer: his works and his audience. New York: Basic, 1971.

Chafe, W. H. The American woman: her changing social, economic, and political roles, 1920-1970. London: Oxford, 1972.

Chafetz, J. S. Masculine, feminine, or human: an overview of the sociology of sex roles. Itasca, Ill.: Peacock, 1974.

Coffin, T. P. The female hero in folklore and legend.
   New York: Simon and Schuster, 1975.

Comstock, G. A., and G. Lindsay. Television and human
   behavior: the research horizon, future and present.
   Santa Monica, Calif.: Rand, 1975.

Davidson, W. P., and W. T. C. Yu (eds.). Mass communication research: major issues and future directions. New York: Praeger, 1974.

Dohrman, R. M. "A gender profile of children's educa-
   tional television," Journal of Communication, 24(4),
   1974, pp. 55-65.

Duberman, L. Gender and sex in society. New York:
   Praeger, 1975.

Dworkin, A. Woman hating. New York: Dutton, 1974.

Ellman, M. Thinking about women. New York: Harcourt
   Brace Jovanovich, 1968.

Farber, S. "Where has all the protest gone? To television," in F. H. Voelker and L. A. Voelker (eds.),
   Mass media: forces in our society. New York: Harcourt Brace Jovanovich, 1975.

Ferguson, M. A. Images of women in literature. Boston:
   Houghton Mifflin, 1977.

Feshbach, S. "Reality and fantasy in filmed violence," in
   J. P. Murray, E. A. Rubinstein, and G. A. Comstock
   (eds.), Television and social behavior. Vol. 2: Television and social learning. Washington, D. C.: Government Printing Office, 1971.

Fielder, L. Love and death in the American novel. New
   York: Stein & Day, 1975.

Filene, P. G. Him/her/self: sex roles in modern America.
   New York: Harcourt Brace Jovanovich, 1975.

Franzblau, S.; J. Sprafkin; and E. Rubenstein. "Sex on
   TV: A content Analysis," Journal of Communication,
   27(2), 1977, pp. 164-170.

Franzwa, H. H. "Working women in fact and fiction," Journal of Communication, 24(2), 1974, pp. 104-109.

Friedan, B. The feminine mystique. New York: Dell, 1963.

Friedrich, L. K. and A. H. Stein. Aggressive and prosocial television programs and the natural behavior of preschool children. Monograph of the Society for Research in Child Development, 38, 1973, pp. 4-12.

Friendly, F. Due to circumstances beyond our control. New York: Random House, 1968.

Gerbner, G. "Violence in television drama: trends and symbolic functions," in G. A. Comstock and E. A. Rubinstein (eds.), Television and social behavior. (Vol. 1). Washington, D.C.: Government Printing Office, 1972.

Greenberg, B. S. Life on television: content analysis of U.S. TV drama. Norwood, N.J.: Ablex, 1980.

_____, and B. Reeves. "Children and the perceived reality of television," Journal of Social Issues, 32(4), 1976, pp. 80-97.

Greenfield, J. "TV is not the world," Television Quarterly, 1978, XV(3), pp. 48-56.

_____. Television: the first fifty years. New York: Abrams, 1977.

Haskell, M. From reverence to rape: the treatment of women in the movies. New York: Holt, Rinehart and Winston, 1974.

Head, S. W. "Content analysis of television drama programs," Quarterly of Film, Radio and Television, 9, 1954, pp. 175-194.

Hicks, D. G. "Imitation and retention of film-mediated aggressive peer and adult models," Journal of Personality and Social Psychology, 4(2), 1965, pp. 97-100.

Inkeles, A. "Society, social structure and child socialization," in J. A. Clausen (ed.), Socialization and society. Boston: Little, Brown, 1968, p. 121.

Isber, C., and M. Cantor. Report of the task force on
women in public broadcasting. Washington, D. C.:
Corp. for Public Broadcasting, 1975.

Jones, M. J. "The spinster detective," Journal of Communication, 25(2), 1975, pp. 106-112.

Jung, C. G. The archetypes and the collective unconscious.
New York: Bollingen, 1959.

_____. Man and his symbols. New York: Dell, 1968.

Kagan, J. "Acquisition and significance of sextyping and
sex role identity," in M. L. Hoffman and L. W. Hoffman (eds.), Review of child development research.
(Vol. 1). New York: Russell Sage, 1964.

Kanin, F. Cited in Bill Froug, The screenwriter looks at
screenwriting. New York: Dell, 1972, p. 128.

Kirkpatrick, J. T. "Homes and homemakers on American
TV," in W. Arens and W. P. Montague (eds.), The
American dimension: cultural myths and social realities.
New York: Alfred, 1976.

Kline, F. G., and P. J. Tichenor (eds.). Current perspectives in mass communication research. Belmont, Calif.:
Sage, 1972.

Lemon, J. "Women and blacks on prime time television,"
Journal of Communication, 27(1), 1977, pp. 70-79.

Levinson, R., and W. Links. Stay tuned: an inside look at
the making of prime time television. New York: St.
Martin's Press, 1981.

Liebert, R. M.; J. M. Neale; and E. S. Davidson. The
early window: effects of television on children and youth.
New York: Pergamon Press, 1973.

Lofland, J. Analyzing social settings: a guide to qualitative
observation and analysis. Belmont, Calif.: Wadsworth,
1971.

Long, M., and R. J. Simon. "The roles and statuses of
women on children and family TV programs," Journalism Quarterly, 51, 1974, pp. 107-110.

Maccoby, E., and C. Jacklin. The psychology of sex differences. Stanford, Calif.: Stanford University Press,
1974.

Mankiewicz, F., and J. Swerdlow. Remote control: television and the manipulation of American life. New York:
New York Times Books, 1978.

McNeil, J. C. "Feminism, feminity, and the television
series: a content analysis," Journal of Broadcasting,
19(3), 1975, pp. 259-271.

Miller, M., and B. Reeves. "Children's occupational sex
role stereotypes: the linkages between television content and perception." A paper presented to the International Communication Association, Chicago, 1975.

_____, and _____. "Dramatic television content and
children's sex role stereotypes," Journal of Broadcasting, 20(1), 1976, pp. 35-47.

Mischel, W. "Sex-typing and socialization," in P. Mussen
(ed.), Carmichael's manual of child psychology. (Vol.
2). New York: Wiley, 1970.

Mussen, P. H. "Early sex role development," in D. A.
Goslin (ed.), Handbook of socialization theory and research. Chicago: Rand McNally, 1969.

Newcomb, H. Television: the most popular art. Garden
City, N.Y.: Anchor, 1974.

_____. "Towards a television aesthetic," in Newcomb
(ed.), The critical view: television. New York: Oxford, 1976, pp. 273-289.

Newsweek, January 19, 1943, cover.

Oakley, A. Women's work: the housewife, past and present. New York: Random House, 1974, p. 60.

Ozersky, R. "Television and intimations of life: social
and thematic patterns in top-rated television dramatic
programs during the period 1950-1970. A descriptive
study" (Doctoral dissertation, New York University,
1976). Dissertation Abstracts International, 37, 1976,
pp. 708A-709A. University Microfilms No. 76-19,042.

Poulos, R. W., E. A. Rubinstein, and R. M. Liebert.
    "Positive social learning," Journal of Communication,
    25(4), 1975, pp. 90-97.

Reinartz, K. F. "The paper doll: images of women in
    popular songs," in J. Freeman (ed.), Women: a femin-
    ist perspective. Palo Alto, Calif.: Mayfield, 1975.

Robinson, M. "Television and perceptions of the world,"
    in D. Cater and R. Adler (eds.), Television as a social
    force: New approaches to TV criticism. New York:
    Praeger, 1975.

Rosen, M. Popcorn Venus: women, movies and the Ameri-
    can dream. New York: Avon, 1973, p. 403.

Seegar, J. F. "Television's portrayal of minorities and
    women, 1971-1975," Journal of Broadcasting, 21, 1977,
    pp. 435-446.

_____, and P. Wheeler. "World of work on TV: Ethnic
    & sex representation in TV drama," Journal of Broad-
    casting, 17, 1973, pp. 201-214.

Sennett, M. "Cloud-cuckoo country," in R. D. MacCann
    (ed.), Film: a montage of theories. New York: Dut-
    ton, 1966.

Shanks, R. The cool fire: How to make it in television.
    New York: Vintage, 1977.

Shulman, A., and Youman, R. How sweet it was: Televi-
    sion, a pictorial commentary. New York: Bonanza,
    1966.

Smythe, D. W. "Reality as presented by television," Public
    Opinion Quarterly, 18, 1954, pp. 143-156.

Sullerot, E. Women, society and change. Trans. by M. S.
    Archer. New York: McGraw-Hill, 1974.

Tedesco, N. "Patterns in prime time," Journal of Commun-
    ication, 24(2), 1974, pp. 119-124.

Trodahl, V. C. "Studies of consumption of mass media con-
    tent," Journalism Quarterly, 42, 1965, pp. 596-606.

Tuchman, G.; A. Kaplan; and J. Benet (eds.). Hearth & home: images of women in the mass media. New York: Oxford University Press, 1978.

Turow, J. "Advising & ordering: daytime, primetime," Journal of Communication, 24(2), 1974, pp. 138-141.

U.S. Commission on Civil Rights. Window dressing on the set: women and minorities in television. Washington, D.C.: U.S. Government Printing Office, 1977.

Wander, P. "Counters in the social drama: some notes on 'All in the Family,'" in H. Newcomb (ed.), The critical view of television. New York: Oxford University Press, 1976.

Ward, S., and M. L. Ray. "Cognitive responses to mass communication: results from laboratory studies and a field experiment." Paper prepared for the Association for Education in Journalism Convention in San Diego, 1974.

Ward, W. D. "Process of sex role development," Developmental Psychology, 9(2), 1969, pp. 163-168.

Warren, C. A. B. Identity and community in the gay world. New York: Wiley, 1974.

Williams, C. T. "It's not so much 'you've come a long way, baby' as 'you're gonna make it after all,'" Journal of Popular Culture, 8(4), 1974, pp. 78-83.

Williams, J. E., and Bennett, S. M. "The definition of sex stereotypes via the adjective check list," Sex Roles, 1(4), 1975, pp. 327-337.

Williams, S. R. Riding the nightmare: women and witchcraft. New York: Atheneum, 1978.

Winnick, C., and Kinsie, P. M. The lively commerce. New York: New American Library, 1972.

Yorburg, B. Sexual identity. New York: Wiley, 1974.

Appendix A ★ THE VIEWER'S CHOICE

Television's Unrealistic Picture of
Life in the U. S. A.

It is obvious that neither the comedies nor the dramatic
genres have shown our society realistically. They have depicted our reactions to social and economic changes, along
with the confusion and frustration we have experienced in
confrontation with a changing society. But episodic television has reflected those changes in society only obliquely,
as it presented an image of our society distorted by the desire for non-change, by an emphasis on tradition, predic-
tion, repetition, stability, and the status quo. A simple
comparison--between social conditions reported in the news
and those portrayed on prime time--demonstrates how un-
representative television's view of society has been.

REPRESENTATIVENESS OF TELEVISION'S
PICTURE OF OUR SOCIETY

In the period between 1950 and 1980 American social and
economic conditions were in almost constant change. The
post-war period introduced massive change in values and
habits of the American people: accelerated urbanization,
improved technology, increased leisure time; civil rights
movements, women's movements, and peace movements;
and revolutions in social patterns of the institutions of family, religion, education, and politics. The increased amount
and uniformity of information made available through the medium of television contributed to a growing awareness of a
sense of instability about basic social institutions and social
landmarks by which Americans gauged the quality of their

lives.   These institutions which formerly provided a sense
of continuity across generations--the church, the family, the
government--were themselves in a process of upheaval and
transformation.

By contrast, however, prime-time entertainment reflected little change or transformation in the basic values
and mores of the American people.   The world presented on
episodic television was mostly unchanging in themes and values from 1950 to 1980.   Similar character types appeared in
dramatic shows of the eighties as had appeared in dramatic
shows of the fifties, and the circumstances and values evident in the 1954 episodes of I Love Lucy shows were echoed
in the 1980 episodes of Laverne and Shirley.

In dramatic formats male dominance was emphasized
and the stigma of anything remotely feminine pervaded frontier and urban locales.   Male occupations on popular programs were predominantly ultra-masculine, 46 percent of
them in fields of crime detection, law enforcement or spy
work.   Violence was valued, as the strong protected the
weak, solving problems by the sword.

In situation comedy, the values associated with wom-
en and the family were relatively unchanged throughout the
thirty-year period.   The responsibility to and reliability of
the family were consistently represented and the stability of
the family unit was subtly argued in episode after episode.
Marriage was presented as a trap for men, a panacea for
women.

An example of unchanging values over a period of
time is seen in discussions about marriage and the sexes in
two situation comedies, one popular in the early 1950's, the
other in the 1970's.   In both series, wives--no longer romantic figures--are seen as the cause of their husband's
confinement.   Ozzie of The Adventures of Ozzie and Harriet
and Archie on All in the Family made disparaging comments
about the entrapment of marriage:

Ozzie: It's gonna be awful lonesome tonight.

Harriet: I'll be here.

Ozzie: I mean, without the boys....

Harriet: David's been seeing a lot of Susan these
            days, do you think it's anything serious?

Ozzie: He's just a boy.

Harriet: And Susan's a girl--that's a good start.
           Besides we were pretty young when we got
           married. In fact, we get younger every
           time you tell about it....

Ozzie: How did David seem when he came home
           [from Susan's] last night? Did he seem
           happy? Sad?

Harriet: He was whistling.

Ozzie: Was it a sad tune?

Harriet: He seemed pretty happy.

Ozzie: He's happy because he doesn't know what
           he's getting into. [1]

                    *   *   *

Gloria: Boy, Michael, when you walked out, I
           didn't think we'd be celebrating a wedding,
           let alone an anniversary.

Michael: Yeah, it was really something. Between
           my Uncle Cass wanting a priest and Archie
           wanting a reverend--

Archie: And you--wanting out.

Michael: I didn't want out--

Archie: You didn't want to get married at all. You
           wanted to go off and live in sin. You
           wanted all the fun and none of the suffering.[2]

In general attitude depicted in these and other situation comedies was a pattern of male characters who grudg-
ingly concede marriage as an inevitable state of confinement
and female characters who are contented in marriage. This
picture of the sexes did not reflect the real state of affairs,
as researchers have repeatedly shown that women are more
likely to be unhappy in marriage than are men. [3]

In other ways, too, the economic and social realities
of the American people were misrepresented on prime time
during this period. Each decade since the coaxial cable was
laid has had a distinctive set of economic and social circumstances affecting our lives--events that appeared in news articles, surveys, and sociological studies. Seldom did they
appear on prime time. The representativeness of what did
appear on prime-time programming is interesting in itself.

THE FIFTIES

In the 1950's, the news was dominated by crisis and turmoil:
coal strikes, steel strikes, rail strikes, communist threats
and Korean casualties.   Economically, the country was faced
with inflation and recession.

There were changes in the circumstances of the American family, as well.   The period between 1950 and 1960
marked the vanguard of the middle-class exodus to the sub-
urbs, and a period of commuting and carpooling for the suburban family.   The average family size also increased substantially in the two decades after the World War, a result
of the "baby boom."

Prime-time characters of the fifties, by contrast,
were largely unaware of deprivation and problems of inflation and recession.   Top-rated dramatic programs of the
decade overwhelmingly depicted financially secure individuals,
and personal economic situations in the comedies reinforced
the picture of comfortable living found in dramatic shows.
The Andersons on Father Knows Best, the two couples on
George Burns and Gracie Allen, the Williams family on
Make Room for Daddy, the Henshaw family on December
Bride and the Nelsons on The Adventures of Ozzie and
Harriet all depicted affluent lifestyles.

Yet the style of living presented on television comedies and dramatic shows presented the pursuit of affluence
without apparent cost to the breadwinners or their families.
While single people were fighting crime and apprehending
lawbreakers, television's married adults spent their time in
the home in leisure pastimes and discussions, not commuting to the city or chauffeuring children to lessons and Little
League.   Not only were there fewer children on television
than in the families of middle class Americans, but television's minors were less evident in the lives of their parents.   Television kids had their own rooms and their own
activities and were seldom bothersome or bored.

Television wives were equally unrealistic.   Although
female employment increased rather than decreased after
World War II, in the media the dominant image of women
was domestic, the preeminent role was that of housewife.
In ads and articles, the emphasis was decidedly on hearth
and home and the housewife's duties to both.   Episodic
television reflected the domestic theme by portraying a

flock of housewives, from Molly Goldberg to <u>Dragnet's</u> Amy
Romero and Fay Smith.

Those female characters who were not housewives
portrayed a sundry assortment of female occupational roles:
secretaries, teachers, maids, entertainers. Almost without
variation, the characters enacting these occupational options
were depicted as misguided, bemused, misfortunate, or immature. Scatterbrained secretaries were included in such
popular programs as <u>My Friend Irma,</u> <u>Private Secretary,</u>
and <u>Meet Millie;</u> distracted teachers were portrayed in <u>Mr.</u>
<u>Peepers</u> and <u>Our Miss Brooks;</u> maids Beulah and Grindl
were seen on series of the same names; and entertainers
constituted other options on <u>Those Whiting Girls</u> and <u>Peter</u>
<u>Gunn.</u> The non-housewives were always unmarried. Thus,
the employed female in episodic television was typically
scatterbrained and single. The counterpart in real life was
far from the media image.

Research statistics presented by sociologists Chafetz
and Sullerot indicated that more than half of the working
women were married in 1950. Moreover, the ratio of married to single employed women increased as the decade wore
on. The greatest increase in the female work force occurred
among well-educated, middle-class, married women--the
same middle-class wives and mothers who were depicted in
the media as contented in domesticity. Employed wives indicated that they worked for the personal satisfaction that resulted from paid recognition of their efforts, as well as the
financial advantages employment afforded. In contrast to the
image of immature, incapable hoydens and misguided maidens
was the typical female worker--a responsible, middle-aged,
married woman, gratified by gainful employment.

Less representative than the working women or suburban families was the presentation of television people almost exclusively as white. Except for Beulah, the black
maid in the series by the same name, no minority women
appeared as regular characters on episodic television of the
fifties. Black men were seen on <u>Amos and Andy</u> and <u>The</u>
<u>Jack Benny Show,</u> and other minority men served as ser-
vants or sidekicks on dramatic formats. In general, however, the population of the videoscape in the first decade
was white, Anglo-American.

THE SIXTIES

Even more explosive than the decade before was the news of
the 1960's.   The Bay of Pigs and the Berkeley Free Speech
Movement altered our images of the military, the police,
and the university student.   Assassinations and riots marked
public gatherings in Brooklyn, Cleveland, Dallas, Miami,
Chicago, Atlanta, and Los Angeles.   It was a decade of
conspicuous contrast: peaceful protesting was followed by
bombings and murder; beautification programs here contrasted
with news of napalming in Viet Nam.

If the news was explosive, the events on prime-time
programs of entertainment were tranquil and fanciful.   Problems on television comedy evolved around the innocent incompetence of country bumpkins and government agents or
the petty tyrannies of unreasonable employers.   Pastoral
settings became popular for the first time and were prominent on a host of popular comedies, including Andy Griffith,
Green Acres, Petticoat Junction, and The Real McCoys.
Fantasy characters abounded, with ghosts, Martians, and
vampires among them.

In real life, change and protest were rife.   The
changes in women's roles were more pronounced than in the
1950's.   By 1965 women accounted for 34 percent of the total work force and more than 60 percent of this group were
married.   Moreover, several scientific studies suggested
that women's expanded economic role substantially influenced
interpersonal relationships within the family and the distribution of domestic responsibilities.   According to these reports,
women and men were more likely to share domestic tasks,
decision-making, and childrearing in households when the
wife had outside employment.

Concurrent with changes in women's status in the
home were media reports of meetings and demonstrations
protesting the second-class status of women in political and
other institutional arenas.   The women's movement was beginning to have an impact.   As early as 1964, women gath-
ered for caucuses and conferences calling for an end to dis-
crimination and issuing a cogent indictment of society's
treatment of women.   "Consciousness-raising" groups and
sisterhood organizations blossomed all over the nation.   By
1966 Betty Friedan's book, The Feminine Mystique, documenting the housewife's malaise and Madison Avenue's response, was a best seller.

The effects of the women's movement went unnoted in 1960's television entertainment. The major change from the previous decade was in the relative absence of prominent female characters in either situation comedy or dramatic series. Many popular situation comedies, such as The Phil Silvers Show, McHale's Navy, Andy Griffith, and Hogan's Heroes, ignored the existence of women altogether, featuring the all-male environs of the military or law enforcement. Top-rated dramatic series that featured no major females included Bonanza, Branded, Combat, Dragnet, Wagon Train, and The Man from UNCLE.

Of the shows in which women were prominent, there was a dearth of female characters with recognizable humanness. Typical 1960's comedy programs depicted fantasy women of superhuman capabilities who lived to serve the man they loved; the list of programs about female vampires, genies, robots, and witches included The Munsters, The Addams Family, I Dream of Jeannie, My Living Doll, and Bewitched. Worlds without women or peopled with supernatural characters who slavishly fulfilled male wishes represented the bulk of popular programming during this decade.

At the same time that the women's movement was influencing beliefs and behaviors of women, many of America's youth were engaged in a social revolution of their own. Rebelling against the mores and morals of their parents, rejecting their values, the young opted for deviant dress and casual lifestyles. News articles showed the young as political protestors taking drugs and living communally. The reaction of the generation who were their parents was bewilderment and anger.

Prime-time programs of the period presented a different picture of relations between the generations. Many of the popular shows dealt with military or police settings which portrayed no children, but those which had children as primary characters generally showed good-natured, obedient offspring, interacting with wise, loving parents. The docile, innocent adolescents who were regular characters on five of the top ten comedies of the decade were a marked contrast to the rebellious young on the seven o'clock news.

The network news continued to focus upon the violent and sensation aspects of all protest movements of the decade: the women's movement, the peace protests, the drug culture and, throughout the decade, the civil rights movement. Although their coverage was criticized by the Kerner Commission as having a white bias, the news reported the civil disturbance and racial strife in black communities of major urban areas. CBS news softened the charges of superficial, biased reporting of the civil rights movement with a seven-part documentary series about black culture and black stereotypes in recent history.

In episodic television, a token nod to the civil rights movement was seen in the dramatic series I Spy in which a black-white relationship between equals was depicted for the first time. In addition, there were occasional roles for black males on professional dramas and regular roles as a member of a team on Ironside, Mission Impossible, and Mod Squad. Asian-Americans were members of the team on Hawaii Five-O. Minority women were almost as scarce as the decade before except for small gains, such as the black secretary on Mannix and minor roles as nurses or receptionists. The exception to this picture was the surprise hit show of 1968, Julia, about a young, widowed black nurse, the mother of a little boy; however, the show was criticized by black groups for saccharin content and a distorted presentation of black family life, which one critic noted was "more in the tradition of Doris Day than Ralph Bunche."[4] It was a criticism which would be equally valid for many of the ethnic portrayals of the next decade, as well.

THE SEVENTIES

The social and political climate of the early 1970's was a continuation of the changes noted in the later years of the preceding decade. War, protest, busing, and bombings were subject matter for news stories. The demonstrations of the young and the civil rights movements continued to capture headlines. Sociologists and medical doctors discussed a revolution in sexual mores.

By the early 1970's women were becoming more militant about their rights, as the level of discontent rose among women in all strata, but especially among the well-educated and employed. Women lobbied and demonstrated for equal pay legislation, union representation, and more positive media representation. The issue of media representation was a particularly sensitive issue to the women's movement and research findings documenting the misrepresentation of women in television, film, and print supported women's complaints. Thus, women's images of themselves began to change and they began to protest the media images of females and of the family.

In the early seventies, the television family of prime-time programs still did not reflect the typical American household. The employed father and house-bound mother of one or more children represented only 19 percent of American households, according to the 1974 Bureau of Labor Statistics. Yet the typical prime-time program still presented this domestic scene. Furthermore, the housewife was still the predominant female role on prime time between 1970 and 1975.

Some change in the depiction of realistic themes was observed at mid-decade. The events of news stories began to be noted in situation comedies for the first time. The generation gap, protest, pollution, inflation, and racial tension were some of the newsworthy subjects of All in the Family episodes and women's liberation was discussed in episodes of Maude, The Mary Tyler Moore Show, and Rhoda, as well as All in the Family.

In addition, there was a greater range of occupational roles for women presented in situation comedies by the mid-seventies. Although housewives still prevailed among role models, series such as The Mary Tyler Moore Show, The Bob Newhart Show, One Day at a Time, Rhoda, Bionic Woman, Charlie's Angels, and Policewoman depicted employed women. The presentation of successful and satisfied career women was innovative for episodic television.

Researchers found, however, that the pattern of male dominance in interpersonal relationships still lingered in the 1970's despite a few exceptional instances portrayed on Maude and Rhoda. Character Mary Richards of The Mary Tyler Moore Show deferred to her male boss when others did not, and Louise Jefferson of The Jeffersons was resistant but controlled by her husband, George. The ambivalence felt toward independent females was perhaps best expressed in quick cancellation of several seventies' series: Sara, Fay, Amy Prentiss, Kate McShane, Karen, Get Christie Love, The Nancy Walker Show, in which females were featured in non-traditional television roles.

Also evident on episodic television of the decade were

obvious attempts to include minorities, particularly male
minorities. Family-centered comedies featuring blacks of
both sexes were seen on such prime-time shows as Good
Times, The Jeffersons, Sanford and Son, and That's My
Mama. On most shows depicting minorities, however, only
minority males were represented: Barney Miller, Chico
and the Man, Hawaii Five-O, On the Rocks, Policewoman,
Welcome Back, Kotter, for example. This last show per-
sonified two ethnic groups in one character named Juan Ep-
stein.

     The ethnicity of television's minority figures was
primarily in their names, and little differentiated them or
identified them with a particular culture. As several analysts
noted, ethnic characters of the seventies could be replaced
by any non-WASPS with little change in characterization;
cynical, lazy Yamana of Barney Miller could be played as
black, chicano, Jewish, or Puerto Rican without loss of the
identifiable features of the character, because the character
was not identifiably ethnic. Television's portrayal of the
ethnic or minority character was a white-washed non-WASP
who lived and worked in harmony with whites. In contrast
to the anger, rage, and bloodshed reported on news formats,
the prime-time picture was of minority people who really
weren't very different--from each other or their white
friends, and who interacted with whites like a member of
the family.

     The reviews summarized here documented the unreal-
ity of the television world. Prime-time pictures of the past
thirty years did not agree with the way we were described
in demographic studies or surveys of social conditions of the
times. Nor did episodic television reflect current events or
the distinctive economic and social characteristics of each
decade. It is apparent that prime-time television has not
been very representative in its portrayal of our society.
Why have viewers made it so popular?

     Prime-time programming was not the only game in
town. In addition to the formulaic fare of predictable characters and unchanging patterns on episodic television, the
medium has offered viewers extraordinary events. It has
presented pictures of human beings walking on the moon, of
formerly hostile enemies signing peace treaties, of master-
pieces of the theatre, film, dance, music, and art worlds.
If audiences preferred the predictability of prime-time episodic programming to televised history and art, it is because
of the peculiar satisfaction prime-time images provided.

In contrast to the chaotic, disordered quality of real life in a state of change, episodic television generally presented a world under control. The predictability of the Western, the formulaic familiarity of the action or comic series, even the ritualized uniformity of sporting events contrasted with changing conditions in everyday life. Situation comedy presented a world in which any dilemma could be resolved in twenty-four minutes and dramatic series showed men of all color united against evil, uncompromising enemies.

The predictability of prime-time television and the order and control it represented likely provided viewers relief from the radical transformation of habits and values, institutions, and social movements of American life. Although prime-time series were repetitious and formulaic they also depicted contemporary issues to some extent. They dealt with personal problems, interpersonal conflicts, social responsibilities. Thus, to the mass audience who responded to the recognizable characters and patterns, these shows provided expression of audience members' own anxieties and frustrations. And they were models for behavior and a glimpse of the way the world works.

NOTES

1.   The Adventures of Ozzie and Harriet; "David's engagement"; Episode No. 27-114; 1957.

2.   All in the Family; "Mike and Gloria's wedding: Part II"; Episode No. 0312; 1972.

3.   See J. Bernard, "The paradox of the happy marriage," in V. Gornick and B. M. Moran (eds.), Women in sexist society: studies in power and powerlessness. New York: Basic Books, 1971.

4.   Fife, M. D. "Black image in American TV: the first two decades," Black Scholar, 6(4), 1974, 13.

Appendix B ★ DESCRIPTIVE LIST OF
SAMPLED SHOWS

1950-1955

BIG TOWN

An early entry in the spy-crime genre was this show about
a crusading newspaper hero, Steve Wilson.   In his struggle
against the legions of crime, corruption, and subversion,
Wilson was aided by city editor Charlie Anderson and by an
adoring sidekick.   Initially the female sidekick was reporter
Lorelei Kilbourne but in 1955 she was replaced by Diane
Walker, a commercial artist.   Other female characters were
wives or victims or wife-victims.

Representative was an episode entitled "The Arsonist," which pits Wilson and associates against a professional
arson ring.   They're led to the ring by a newly made widow
whose husband was killed in a fire he started himself.
Charlie, posing as a business executive, contacts the ring
and arranges a fire, while Steve Wilson arranges for a police audience at the event.   The arsonists outsmart them,
however, by holding hostage the businessman's (Charlie's)
wife until the successful completion of their contract.   On a
hunch, Wilson sends Charlie to the apartment, where he confronts the kidnapper-arsonist and utters a plea which becomes
a cliché for scores of programs to come: "My wife. Let
her go.   I'll stay, [I don't care what you do to me], but let
her go."   The arsonist isn't so chivalrous but rescue is at
hand moments later in the persons of Wilson and the police.
Criminals are apprehended, wives are restored to their own
homes and the noble crusader rests.   The show aired from
1950 to 1956.

I LOVE LUCY

A prime-time classic was created around the marriage of a
willful, rambunctious child-woman and her beleaguered enter-
tainer-husband.   Besides the harassed husband Ricky Ricardo,
Lucy's companions were co-conspirator Ethel and her husband, Fred.   The incompetent, incorrigible, and impulsive
Lucy Ricardo was an ideal comic figure and Lucille Ball's
incomparable artistry raised the show to the level of art.
It debuted on October 15, 1951, and by its final prime-time
airdate, I Love Lucy had won hundreds of awards, including
five Emmys and a Peabody.

        The show had the additional distinction of introducing
pregnancy to prime time and vice versa.   Lucille Ball,
pregnant with her second child, enacted the role of expectant
Lucy with heartfelt believability.   In due time Ricky Ricardo,
Jr. was born on prime time, coinciding to the day with
Ball's delivery of her own son.   It was a banner event,
heralded by Life, Newsweek, Time, and Walter Winchell.

        In "Baby Pictures," filmed two months later, Lucy
was characteristically exaggerated in the pose of proud parent.   The central conflict arose between two mothers, Lucy
and Carolyn Appleby, as to whose baby was superior in looks
or breeding.   Lucy remarks to Ethel, "I feel like a mother
bear defending her cub!" and Ethel responds, "I guess all's
fair in love and motherhood."   The impact of Lucy as mother
was considerably diminished, however, by the drama of the
competition.   Lucy dresses her young son in new clothes to
parade before Carolyn and both mothers deposit their charges
in a playpen to better attend to the verbal duel between them.
Although the plot supposedly evolves around mother love, in
only one scene are the women shown "mothering" their chil-
dren--a minute and a half in which they are shown tentative-
ly holding their babies on their laps as they argue over the
child's accomplishments.

        Thus, in spite of the heralds and the hoopla, I Love
Lucy featured weak images of new motherhood.   There were
few stories about parenting, childcaring, or postpartum feelings.   Instead, the stories continued to explore the limits
Ricky would endure or to which Lucy would go to express
herself, preferably in show business.

DRAGNET

This long-running series introduced documentary-type voice-over and a realistic depiction of police work to the spy-crime audience. Jack Webb, the creative inspiration on both sides of the camera, opened each program with a terse narration as city street scenes played: "This is the city. Los Angeles, California. I work here. I'm a cop." Music contributed to the sense of drama in the step-by-step procedures of the investigative case which followed.

The dispassionate sergeant Joe Friday and his partner, Frank Smith, plodded through the monotonous, dangerous, and banal work of the Los Angeles Police Department week after week in search of "the facts, ma'am." At the end of the episode viewers were informed of the results of the investigation, including the site of the trial and the severity of the sentence, as the actor who had played the criminal stood impassive before the camera. It was an extraordinary show, opening on January 3, 1952, and playing prime time for more than ten years.

The unemotional style of the show permeated the episode about New Year's Eve filmed in the mid-fifties. The story concerned the several notable cases Friday and Smith had covered during the past year along with noncommittal comments about their work, its cost to their personal lives, and the public's ignorance of their contribution. It began and ended with a New Year's Eve party at Smith's house where the festivity carries on in another room as the two partners indulge in reverie and quiet celebration.

THE LIFE OF RILEY

The models for the bumbling husband-father, wise wife, and children with names like Babs and Junior were presented on this series. Chester Riley found himself mucking the stew at every well-meant intervention in his private and family affairs, and mumbling "What a revolting turn of events this is" at every unfortunate turn of events. Peg, his wife, was ever-patient and supportive.

1955-1960

THE ADVENTURES OF OZZIE AND HARRIET

Notable for its fourteen-year run on prime time, this comedy was also distinguished by the circumstance of showing
the principals playing themselves: Ozzie and Harriet Nelson
and their sons, David and Ricky, were actually members of
the same family.   Furthermore, the easy pace of the show
and the ordinary problems of its characters gave it a realistic tone, only somewhat diminished by Ozzie's pratfalls and
mishaps.

Typical elements were seen on an episode filmed in
1957 entitled, "David's Engagement."   The story evolves
around Ozzie's erroneous conclusion that son David is on
the brink of marriage to his girlfriend.   A series of coin-
cidental events appear to confirm the parents' concern that
his elopement is imminent.   In the final scene Ozzie and
Harriet rush to the justice of the peace (the former bound-
ing down stairs and into walls), only to learn that David has
gone there to pay a speeding ticket.   All is well.

GUNSMOKE

This show and The Life and Legend of Wyatt Earp, both introduced the same week, were the vanguard of the adult
Western.   "Adult" in this context apparently meant an emphasis on weaponry and violent confrontation in the opening
credits, although, in the case of Gunsmoke the violence was
disclaimed by the hero's grimace as he fired on his oppo-
nent.   The series concerned four regulars in Dodge City:
the stalwart marshall, Matt Dillon; Miss Kitty, owner of the
Longbranch Saloon; Chester, Dillon's deputy noted for a limp
and a twang and the devotion of a slave; and crusty but lov-
able "Doc."

It was a clan of sorts, headed by the 6'7" hero,
played by James Arness.   The clan's enemy was the outlaw,
the bully, the misfit whose presence disrupted the community.   In "Five Painted-Up Chippies," the enemy is a lawless
gang threatening peace and prosperity ($48,000 worth of
gold).   The outlaw gang planned to rob a band of "fancy ladies" migrating to Dodge City.   Dillon sabotages their efforts
but not before such events as a hairpulling fight between two

of the fancy ladies and a reunion between one prostitute and a waif who may be her son.   The outlaws are disposed of, the fancy ladies are saved, and order and calm descend on Dodge.   The series lasted twenty years.

THE RIFLEMAN

The rifleman, Lucas McCain, was a Western hero not unlike Matt Dillon.   He destroyed or disbanded the various desperadoes who threatened the town while guiding a protégé (his motherless son, Mark) in the ways of the world.   In these endeavors, he depends upon canny insight, strong will, and his .44-40 Winchester rifle.

A typical episode in the second season involves passengers on a train, including two characters other than the McCains--an old man, formerly a buffalo hunter and a convicted killer on his way to his own execution.   The killer's comrades ambush and command the train.   The buffalo hunter at first fails to live up to his boasts to Mark but with McCain's boldness and the boy's miserable eyes to give him courage, he and Lucas together outshoot the attackers.   The buffalo hunter dies, however, and Lucas and Mark go on to their destination.

DECOY

As familiar as the barren frontier was to Matt Dillon and Lucas McCain, the urban ghettos were the milieu for Casey Jones.   Beverly Garland was Jones, a New York City police officer in a series which resembled Dragnet in its narrative style.   Each week Jones presented the highlights of an investigation in which the policewoman figured prominently.   Sometimes it was a tribute to the dedication of police officers, as in "Fiesta at Midnight" in which Jones perseveres in a wearying attempt to find a witness, a young Hispanic falsely accused of murder.   "When a life is at stake, we don't like to give up," Jones explains in the voice-over.

MAVERICK

Not a gunfighter but a gambler and a ladies man, this hero was an exception, a maverick.   James Garner played Bret Maverick, "living on jacks and queens" as he wandered the

West, avoiding mayhem and peril whenever possible and quoting philosophical observations of his "pappy." In the 1958-1959 season he enjoyed an on-going feud with Samantha Crawford, a riverboat gambler, love interest, and con artist. He was also joined by brother Bart on numerous episodes.

The spoof on Westerns extended to wordplays, such as towns called Hounddog, Bent Forks, and Oblivion; a femme fatale named Caprice; and dialogue like these lines from "Point Blank": "Maverick, you've got ten minutes to get out of this town." "Sheriff, I've gotten out of towns this size in five minutes." As the lines suggest, when Maverick did act the hero, as he did here, the apprehended robbers include the sheriff's girlfriend and his deed brings him little applause or esteem. He's better off squandering his youth, pursuing lady luck, "the lady he loves best."

THE ANN SOTHERN SHOW

A prototype for the independent careerwoman, championed twelve years later in The Mary Tyler Moore Show, Katy O'Connor was assistant manager of Bartley House, a New York hotel. The lead, played by Ann Sothern, was involved in the day-to-day grievances of running a big city hotel to the satisfaction of its manager, Jason Macauley, and the hotel quests. Katy's friend and roommate, Olive Smith, and bellboy Johnny did their parts. A sample episode concerned Katy's difficulties in pleasing the overbearing, overweight Mrs. Macauley, pampering temperamental musicians performing in the ballroom, and gracefully resisting the amorous advances of a hotel guest. The series aired on CBS from 1958 to 1961.

1960-1965

BONANZA

The Western clan suggested by the closely knit relationships seen on Gunsmoke was explored formally within the Cartwright homestead. There the saga of widower Ben Cartwright and his sons, Adam, "Hoss," and Little Joe, was played against the background of their thousand-square-acre Nevada ranch, lending color and a sense of history to the

story.   The color was also real; this was the first episodic
Western broadcast in color.

The beautiful Ponderosa Ranch served an all-male
clan.   All the Cartwrights, the ranchhand, Candy, and the
cook, Hop Sing, were male.   The masculine flavor of other
Westerns was exaggerated on Bonanza where women were an
intrusion, almost a threat to the stability of the masculine
world.   The intrusive feminine influence was always eliminated, however.   Patriarch Ben, the story went, had buried
three wives.   Each of the sons of these unions was attracted
at one time or another to a woman, yet in episode after
episode, the attraction proved fatal, or at best, ill-advised.
The conclusions of these stories uniformly resulted in the
death of the unfortunate lady or her return to a less hostile
environment.   "This is no place for a woman" was a cliché
on the frontier--one given meaning on episodes of Bonanza.

Thus, the Ponderosa continued to be a male society.
The tale of the intrusive female was explicit on an episode
called "The Trap."   It happened that Little Joe innocently
inspired infatuation in Hallie Shannon, a situation which
drives her husband to a murderous rage.   He ambushes
Little Joe but is shot and killed himself in the attack.
Hallie is fairly delighted with the turn of events and pro-
poses marriage immediately after her husband's funeral.
This makes Little Joe uncomfortable and the victim's brother downright suspicious.   The Shannon brother becomes abusive when Hallie and he are alone and she runs out into the
night, only to fall down a cliff and be killed.   Even the ter-
rain conspired against the female who disturbed the masculine community of Bonanza.

DR. KILDARE

Based on the MGM films, this hit series offered all the
elements of the professional drama: male mentor and male
neophyte in an impersonal professional institution.   In this
case the setting was Blair Hospital, with James Kildare as
the neophyte and Dr. Leonard Gillespie as his mentor.   The
hero was idealistic and virtuous, if somewhat deficient in
patience, humility, and restraint.

Kildare's sense of himself was indicated on a 1964
episode, "One for the Road."   The young intern shows dis-
gust when confronted with an incoherent drunk, and anger

that he himself is assigned to a new ward for alcoholics.
An older doctor, a reformed alcoholic, convinces Kildare
that alcoholism is a disease and that these new patients
should be respected.   Won over, Kildare has a change of
heart but it doesn't make him empathetic.   He corrects a
hard-boiled, gray-haired nurse: "I think it might be a good
idea if you got used to calling them alcoholic patients....
I told Dr. Probeck you were a good nurse, don't make a
liar out of me." He is an intern and she a seasoned nurse,
but righteousness is his.   The story continues as several of
the special patients return to drinking and the reformed alcoholic doctor is tempted himself until Kildare wins him
back for sobriety.

THE DICK VAN DYKE SHOW

This situation comedy of the early 1960's employed the same
gags and complications of other comedies, but it bested them
in execution and in warmth.   Its characters were comedy
writer Rob Petrie, married to Laura Petrie; the son, Ritchie;
Rob's colleagues, Sally and Buddy; and producer Mel Cooley.
Together they created the fictional Alan Brady Show and a
much loved situation comedy.

        An example of the show's characteristic portrayal of
marital affection was the episode "The Necklace," in which
Rob is duped by a salesman into buying a gaudy necklace as
a present for his wife.   When presented with the necklace,
Laura reacts with apparent appreciation but confides her dis-
may to her friend Millie Halper.   Rob's parents arrive and
his mother fairly faints with awe and envy upon seeing the
necklace.   Laura offers her the necklace and Rob is never
the wiser.   The time was 1961, our innocent past.

BEVERLY HILLBILLIES

This popular comedy of the decade was based on the propo-
sition that a family of mountaineers who strike oil would
subsequently want to strike out for California.   The Clampett family does just that, leaving the country scenery, if
not their backwoods concepts and customs, behind them.
Daisy Moses, known as "Granny," her son-in-law, Jed
Clampett, his daughter, Elly Mae, and nephew Jethro comprised the rich hillbillies.   Granny's willful independence
and the clan's idiosyncratic methods of dealing with the

stiff-necked socialites of Beverly Hills lead to many of the problems the Clampetts encounter. The problem is usually solved by the sensible Jed, who mollifies the authorities, makes peace with the neighbors, or adapts Granny's old-fashioned methods to modern times.

One episode revealed the Clampett's bewildering confrontation with Southern California as they prepare Jethro for military service by taking him to Marineworld. Once there, Granny fishes for whales, Elly Mae dives into the cement swimming hole with the dolphins, and Jethro skins, cooks, and eats what he has been given to feed the sharks. Jed finally gets everybody out, some dripping, all leaving confusion behind them.

BIG VALLEY

A family dynasty in the late nineteenth century was the background story in this Western. The Barkley ranch, many times the size of the Ponderosa (Bonanza), was ruled by widow Victoria Barkley and her eldest sons, Nick and lawyer Jarrod. The tribe also included their sister, Audra, and Heath, an illegitimate son of the deceased Tom Barkley. In spite of their strength and evident prosperity the Barkleys were often threatened; the women were kidnapped, the men framed or swindled. Central California seemed to be a lawless place in the 1870's.

"Teacher of Outlaws" was a case in point. The story is peopled with outlaws and posses, punctuated with chases and gunfights. Mistaking her for the schoolteacher, the outlaws kidnap Victoria and bring her to their hideout, so she can teach their leader to read and write. In the meantime some outlaw members return from a shoot-out in town; they require a doctor's attention, so one is kidnapped and brought to the hideout. With Victoria's help the doctor effects an escape and eventually leads the posse back to the scene, leading to another shoot-out. The final scene is Victoria at the gravesite of the outlaw leader, whom she taught to read and write and whom she learned to like a little.

BEWITCHED

This ABC hit starred Elizabeth Montgomery as a good witch married to a mortal, an advertising man. Samantha Stevens, the witch, was possessed of the power to control the mortal world around her; she could cast spells, create illusions, transcend time and space. Husband Darrin found this uncomfortable, however, and repeatedly urged her to refrain from witchlike behavior and act like a wife. This basic conflict between the superior person she could be and the submissive image he wanted was further illuminated in the clash between her family (witches and warlocks) and his.

The volatile Endora, Samantha's mother, was a particularly explosive intrusion in the home, for Endora's disapproval and resentment of Darrin were ill-disguised. Darrin's reactions to Endora's hostility were expressions of the baffling contradiction of her position: "I know your mother doesn't care about me, but what about you and the kids?" For Endora's part, however, Darrin was merely a symbol, the mortal who ruled her daughter's affections; his identity was unimportant, as she indicated often by her failure to remember correctly his name.

Samantha's father, Maurice, was no less trouble than Endora although his visitations were infrequent. One visit, an unscheduled appearance to see his new grandson, was the talk of a 1967 episode. It begins with Endora materializing to warn Samantha of her father's impending appearance. Mother and daughter worry what havoc Maurice might wreak when he learns that his grandson is not a namesake. Maurice appears, dismisses Endora, and traps Darrin in an entry hall mirror. Darrin's parents arrive. Samantha tries her magic to release Darrin but Maurice's magic is better, so she invents a story about the entry hall mirror for Darrin's parents. Then she takes Maurice aside and with sweet words and quick talk persuades him of the advantages of her son's name, Adam. He lets Darrin get out of the mirror at about this time, too.

FAMILY AFFAIR

One of the numerous single-father comedies which prospered in the late 1960's was this show. In the five years it aired, viewers had ample opportunity to observe Bill Davis, the affluent adoptive father of three, as he demonstrated indulgent concern at the efforts and trials of Jody, Buffy, and Cissy. Besides their Uncle Bill, the children had another substitute father in Giles French, the Davis's valet. Perhaps it was the forthright sensibility of these male models which caused

them to act so mature but the children did show a remark-
able sensitivity to and philosophical understanding of adults.

For his part, Uncle Bill was also sensitive and understanding. In one story he confronts the eighteen-year-old
Cissy when he learns that she plans to marry because of
peer pressure. He does so in a thoroughly restrained way,
meeting her boyfriend and later reasoning with her: "Greg's
a nice boy ... but you're getting married for the wrong reason." No tantrums here.

MISSION IMPOSSIBLE

In the age of moonwalks and multiple satellites, it was perhaps time that modern technology got its own prime-time
series and this was it. The real draw of this show was
computer-processed information and the electronic gadgets
which weekly penetrated the security stronghold of some unfriendly foreign government. Its human components were
the business-like agent in charge of the operation, Mr.
Phelps; Barney Collier, the wizard of electronic devices;
Rollin Hand, the expert at disguises; Cinnamon Carter, the
attractive distractor; and Willie Armitage, the strong arm,
with muscle and derring-do. With sophisticated technology,
split-second timing, and an assortment of uniforms, the
team successfully completed each week's impossible mission.

Eventually unfriendly governments had all been penetrated and the team turned its talent to crime and terrorism
in the United States. In one such example, the challenge
was to find and defuse a bomb set by a terrorist group
which unites a deranged scientist and some professional as-
sassins in a plot against the population of Los Angeles. The
challenge is met and the team succeeds, almost at the buz-
zer.

THAT GIRL

One of the first of a trend in series about a career woman
who lives alone, the story of a naive, aspiring actor prefigured the more sophisticated version of the seventies.
Ann Marie wanted to become a star, impress her parents,
and marry her boyfriend, Don Hollinger. Like Lucy Ricardo, she was starstruck, dreaming of bright lights and applause. More talented than Lucy, she was still an outsider.

In an episode in which a successful friend asks her to be an
understudy, she is ingenuous in her enthusiasm: "What shall
I wear? My pink suit! Last time I was in a theatre, I
wore an usher's outfit. "

IRONSIDE

The team of crimefighters resembled others of the decade:
two appealing young men--one of them black--and an attractive woman.   Only the leader was different; former San
Francisco police chief Ironside was confined to a wheel-
chair, crippled by a sniper's bullet.   The team's base of
operations was in an unused portion of police headquarters
and there Sergeant Ed Brown, Mark Sanger, and policewoman Eve Whitfield planned strategy with "the chief. "
Ironside participated actively, his mobility increased by use
of a specially equipped police van.

         In "Good Will Tour" Ironside and the team attend a
black tie affair in the line of duty.   The duty apparently
consists of protecting from harm a foreign dignitary, a
prince, and it falls naturally to Whitfield when the prince
shows an interest in her.   She escorts the prince on a
night tour of the town, dancing and sightseeing while the
chief and other teammates follow discreetly, warding off
abusive photographers and would-be attackers.   At dawn
the prince leaves, charmed by Whitfield, pleased by the
tour, and safe and sound.   Cinderella returns to headquarters.

THE GHOST AND MRS. MUIR

The forerunner for Alice, Ann Romano, Elaine Nardo and
other successful women heroes of the 1970's and 1980's
was Carolyn Muir.   Like them, she was a single parent,
a working mother.   She worked as a writer and cared for
her two children, Candice and Jonathon, and their dog,
Scruffy, in a picturesque bungalow, Gull Cottage, overlook-
ing Schooner Bay in New England.   In this she was aided
by a housekeeper named Martha Grant and impeded by Captain Daniel Gregg, the ghost of Gull Cottage.

         The ghost is a handsome figure of a nineteenth-
century sea captain and although he resents the intrusion at
Gull Cottage, he eventually becomes fond--even jealous--of

Carolyn Muir. In "Mr. Perfect" an old beau from the city
comes to capture Carolyn's affections and the Captain is
agitated. His interference is not subtle--cognac spills, pictures fall on the poor fellow--and Carolyn becomes angry:
"What I feel for Blair is between him and me and nobody
else and I'm warning you, don't try to embarrass him
again." Carolyn Muir also shows her independence in resisting the "perfect" Blair in marriage, choosing her life
at Gull Cottage instead. Although Hope Lange won an Emmy
for her role in 1970, the show was cancelled that year.

MANNIX

Mannix was prominent in a long line of television detectives
who lived by their wits and their fists. In the original
premise Joe Mannix worked for a sophisticated detective
firm dependent upon the electronic instruments of crime
prevention and detection, but his style and temperament were
that of the loner who works without gadgets, so by the second season he had gone into business on his own. His secretary, an attractive black woman named Peggy Fair, was
his only human contact, outside of clients and thugs. Of
the latter there were more than enough and they and Mannix accounted for a notable number of bashes, car crashes,
brawls, broken limbs, and deaths on prime time from 1967
to 1975.

MARCUS WELBY, M.D.

Marcus Welby served a social function similar to that of
Walter Cronkite: his news was often bad but his manner
said things will get better. Welby served in the medical
profession where bad news ran to cancer, blindness, paralysis and strokes, but his calm and his caring concern
helped in the healing. Furthermore, also similar to Cronkite, he looked like somebody's father, somebody's fantasy
father, and that helped, too.

     He worked with a young doctor, Steven Kiley, and an
office nurse, Consuelo Lopez, distinguished for decades as
the only regular Chicana character on prime time. With
the assistance of these two, Welby offered a general practice which turned back the hands of the clock. He made
house calls; discussed fears, furies, and family influences
with troubled patients; and counseled the addicted and the

dying. He and his methods were old-fashioned--humanistic,
holistic--and his lesson to the brilliant young Kiley was that
often those methods are best. In "Go Ahead and Cry" his
gentle probing helps Consuelo discover and recover from depression after a hysterectomy. In another episode his insistent attention forces a Catholic nun to take care of her own
diseased body to be better able to serve other people. In
both stories and in many other episodes, Welby treats the
whole person, body and mind, like the general practitioner
of years gone by, relaying the message that the old ways
are superior to the new.

MEDICAL CENTER

Premiering one day after Marcus Welby and running four
months longer, Medical Center was the longest running medical program on prime-time television. Like Marcus Welby,
the show had two prominent doctors, Joe Gannon and Paul
Lochner, as the young and the experienced, respectively.
The regular characters also included numerous women,
Nurse Wilcox, Nurse Chambers, and Dr. Jeanne Bartlett
among them. However, most women characters were patients, many with problems of the heart as well as the
physique. In a representative sample, Phoebe has breast
cancer and suicidal feelings because of it, for an operation
may save her life but it will end her career as a call girl.
She fails to see that Sam, a doctor friend of Gannon and
Lochner, loves her in spite of her past and her future.
Gannon helps her to see that Sam loves her and her social
and medical prognosis improves.

THE MARY TYLER MOORE SHOW

Signalling new heights in the situation comedy format, The
Mary Tyler Moore Show broadcast the first episode in Sep-
tember 1970. Its characters were realistic, fully drawn
approximations of themselves: Mary Richards, in her early
30's, unmarried, ambitious; Lou Grant, explosive, dedicated
producer of a local news broadcast; Murray Slaughter, sensitive, satiric, intelligent, a news writer; Ted Knight, the
self-indulgent "star" of the news show; Rhoda Morgenstern,
Mary's neighbor and friend; and Phyllis Lindstrom, their
landlady. In 1973 Sue Ann Nivens arrived to star in her
own show, "The Happy Homemaker." The show had won
more than twenty-five Emmys when the participants elected
to end the series in 1977.

One of the contributions The Mary Tyler Moore Show
made was its treatment of women's sexuality on prime time.
Its characters were products of a specific history and had
known the effects of the "sexual revolution" and the women's
movement: Mary has a healthy sexuality, takes birth control
pills; Lou is a casualty of the raised consciousness of his own
wife, Edie, who first separates from and then divorces him;
Murray honestly addresses his own motivations when he
pressures his wife to have another child in "Murray Makes
Three"; and all of the female characters--Mary, Rhoda,
Georgette, Sue Ann, Phyllis--strive for growth and fulfillment, encumbered by their own attitudes and limitations and
hindered at times by male disapproval and resentment.

ALL IN THE FAMILY

Another breakthrough comedy show appeared one year after
The Mary Tyler Moore Show.   Its topics were even more
controversial, the realities which impinged on its characters
more brutal.   The protagonists struggled to comprehend and
survive a changing world which included robbery, rape, and
racial unrest, along with the generation conflicts and family
misunderstandings that comprised the dream of most situation comedies.   Protagonists were Archie Bunker, a bigoted
dock worker; Edith Bunker, a Queens housewife; their daughter, Gloria; and her liberal-student husband, Michael Stivic.

The series was peopled with many other regular
characters, featured in various episodes.   In one episode
Archie and Edith argue about their neighbors, the Lorenzos;
Frank Lorenzo, who can cook, and Irene Lorenzo, who is
mechanically able and good at shooting pool, are threatening
influences in Archie's circle, since not only Gloria but also
Edith is impressed by the Lorenzos.   Equally disturbing are
the Jeffersons, black neighbors whom Edith and the Stivics
befriend.   Louise Jefferson and Edith support and counsel
each other in spite of the antagonism of the two husbands
and when Archie is laid off from work, it is Louise's practical, sympathetic advice that Edith seeks.

THE STREETS OF SAN FRANCISCO

This entry in the spy-crime genre combined successful elements: the new with the experienced professional and a romantic urban setting (familiar to crime show viewers since
The Lineup).   The professionals were police officers Lt.

Mike Stone, the twenty-year veteran, and Inspector Steve
Keller, a vigorous but unwise youngster. Together they
tackled the criminals of San Francisco. In one episode the
criminal is an accomplished "hit-man" named Sidney, who
proves to be a young woman Keller is dating. By mid-
seventies television women were entering all sorts of pro-
fessions.

MAUDE

As controversial as its parent series, All in the Family,
was this descendant, based on a middle-aged, middle-class
liberal who first appeared as Edith Bunker's cousin. Maude
Findlay lived in Westchester County, New York, in comfortable circumstances with her fourth husband, Walter, and
next door to her best friends, Arthur and Vivian. The
Findlays had a housekeeper and Maude's daughter and grandson living with them, too. But for the fire and dynamism of
the female lead and the provocative subject matter, the series might have been one of the bland, conventional comedies
about affluent, suburban families of past eras.

Maude was never bland or conventional. In early seg-
ments the series probed liberal hypocrisy and pomposity and
later it focused on political activism, alcoholism, abortion,
depression, mental health. In several memorable episodes
the show saw the Findlays get a trial separation, experience
loneliness and feelings of failure, and then reconcile. In
1978 the star of the series, Bea Arthur, decided to give up
the part of the dominant, domineering Maude and the series
was ended.

M*A*S*H

This comedy set in South Korea on the war front, which
considered such topics as military casualties, death, and
the futility of war, was necessarily an enrichment of the
comic television format. The humor arose from the personalities of the characters, as in The Mary Tyler Moore
Show, as much as from the situations in which they found
themselves. Many of the personalities were finely tuned
comic types whom the viewer just happened to find in an
army medical company under siege in the Korean War.
Prime among them were the surgeons, Captains Hawkeye
Pierce and Trapper McIntyre and the effete Major Frank

Burns; their commanding officer; the Colonel's aide, a childlike Radar O'Reilly; the amazon head of nurses, Major Margaret Houlihan; and a young Corporal who dressed like a
woman in hopes of earning a discharge.

It was evidently the stuff of comedy and yet the realistic medical operating conditions and the perspective of
tragic human waste in war made the humor sardonic and
bittersweet.   The viewer was made aware that the humor
was what kept the members of the MASH company from becoming casualties of the war themselves.   In "Spring Fe-
ver," for example, characters seek romance with sometimes
improbable partners to alleviate the feelings that war and
sacrifice engender.   In all cases there was a subtle combination of human qualities--of heroic endurance and defeat,
of fear and laughter, of tenderness and guilt.   It combined
some of the best elements of the comic with some of the
best elements of traditional dreams.

POLICEWOMAN

Sgt. Pepper Anderson was the undercover policewoman,
whose team members were detectives Joe Styles and Pete
Royster.   Their superior officer was a solicitous lieutenant,
Bill Crowley.   In a typical story the team investigated criminal conspiracy in the city of Los Angeles, with Pepper posing as a prostitute at some point in the investigations.   Anderson was played by Angie Dickinson.

CHARLIE'S ANGELS

The ratings hit of the 1976 season was a show which featured three female undercover detectives, posing as various
personalities in tennis shorts and bikinis.   The three were
employees of a detective agency owned by Charles Townsend,
whose unseen presence was known through the telephone,
which he used to relay instructions and advice to the three.
Their male associate Bosley aided them, not only listening
to the phone machine but also by joining them on most of
their assignments.

Sabrina was the quick, thoughtful angel, Kelly was
chic and sophisticated, and Jill was the athletic type.   Far-
rah Fawcett Majors, who played Jill, created a national fad
with her long, tousled blond hair.   Cheryl Ladd, who re-

placed her as Jill's younger sister, and Jaclyn Smith as
Kelly were media sensations also.   The appeal of the show
was probably the actors' physical beauty and the opportuni-
ties that the series presented for viewing them in skimpy
apparel.   The opening segment took place at a resort, for
example, and subsequent episodes occurred at recreation
spots, circuses, and beaches.

ALICE

The female hero was a widow who aspired to a singing career.   In the meantime she worked as a waitress at Mel's
Cafe in Phoenix to support herself and her son.   There she
finds her second family: the gruff, but caring Mel and the
other waitresses--brassy Flo and simple, impressionable
Vera.   Stories concern Alice's efforts to fulfill her ambi-
tions, rear her son, and be a friend to Flo, Mel, and Vera.

LAVERNE AND SHIRLEY

Life in the 1950's for two single women with little prestige,
property, or education was the basis for this situation comedy.   Laverne De Fazio and Shirley Feeney, worked in a
brewery and struggled to better themselves.   Laverne's
father owned a pizza place where the two sometimes met
friends, including neighbors Squiggy and Lenny.   Slapstick
comedy, especially with the last two characters, was the
bulk of the show's humor.   The comic sequences sometimes resembled vaudeville routines, as in a toothache episode in which Lenny and Squiggy's elaborate endeavor to
pull Laverne's tooth provides the laughs.

HART TO HART

Two popular television actors, Robert Wagner and Stefanie
Powers, starred in this spy-crime series about a pair of
married sleuths, both rich and sexy.   Lionel Stander was
Max, their worldly valet.   The dangerous escapades of
Jonathan and Jennifer Hart and their glamorous private life
caught the public fancy and the program did well in audience
ratings.   The rapport and affection between the Harts contributed to their attractiveness and the overt sensuality of
their married relationship was a new image for prime-time
television.

On a sample episode the Harts track a suspected
killer to a popular ski resort, a locale which allows them
a hot tub, a sleigh ride, and a race down the slopes.   When
the suspect himself is killed, suspicion shifts to his wife and
girlfriend, and the girlfriend's demise leaves only the wife.
She is the one and jealousy is the motive.   It's a thin plot
but the Harts and the show are lovely together.

Nivens, Sue Ann (The Mary
    Tyler Moore Show) 51, 111,
    174-5

O'Connor, Katy (The Ann
    Sothern Show) 166
O'Reilly, Radar (M*A*S*H)
    54, 177

Paladin (Have Gun--Will Travel)
    109
Petrie, Laura (The Dick Van
    Dyke Show) 43-5, 111, 125,
    168
Petrie, Ritchie (The Dick Van
    Dyke Show) 168
Petrie, Rob (The Dick Van Dyke
    Show) 44, 56, 125, 168
Phelps, Mr. (Mission Impossi-
    ble) 171
Pierce, Hawkeye (M*A*S*H)
    53, 176
Purcell, Beth (Cimarron City)
    41
Pynchon, Margaret (Lou Grant)
    100

Reichman, Ma (Bonanza) 105
Ricardo, Little Ricky (I Love
    Lucy) 3, 5, 162
Ricardo, Lucy (I Love Lucy)
    21-7, 32, 42, 100, 109,
    111, 126, 162, 171
Ricardo, Ricky (I Love Lucy)
    22, 24, 26, 32, 162
Richards, Mary (The Mary
    Tyler Moore Show) 46, 51,
    56, 100, 122, 158, 174-5
Riley, Chester (Life of Riley)
    163
Riley, Peg (Life of Riley) 163
Roger (I Dream of Jeannie) 98
Rogers, Sally (The Dick Van
    Dyke Show) 44-5, 46, 56,
    168
Romano, Ann (One Day at a
    Time) 46, 172
Romero, Amy (Dragnet) 154
Royster, Pete (Policewoman)
    78, 177

Russell, Kitty (Gunsmoke) 89-
    90, 94, 164

Sabrina (Charlie's Angels) 30,
    80, 105, 177
"Sam" (Richard Diamond) 41,
    110
Sanger, Mark (Ironside) 172
Scott, Milly (Rifleman) 41
Serena (Bewitched) 112
Shannon, Hallie (Bonanza) 86,
    89, 167
Slaughter, Murray (The Mary
    Tyler Moore Show) 174-5
Smith, Fay (Dragnet) 38, 154
Smith, Frank (Dragnet) 38,
    57, 58, 163
Smith, Olive (The Ann Sothern
    Show) 166
Sorrell, Buddy (The Dick Van
    Dyke Show) 168
Spencer, Jeff (77 Sunset Strip) 74
Squiggy (Laverne and Shirley) 178
Stevens, Darrin (Bewitched)
    96-8, 112, 170
Stevens, Joan (I Married Joan)
    42
Stevens, Samantha (Bewitched)
    96-8, 109, 112, 127, 169-70
Stivic, Gloria (All in the Fam-
    ily) 46, 49, 130, 152, 175
Stivic, Michael (All in the Fam-
    ily) 46, 130, 152, 175
Stone, Lt. Mike (Streets of San
    Francisco) 61, 66, 176
Street, Della (Perry Mason) 41
Styles, Joe (Policewoman) 78,
    177

Tate, Larry (Bewitched) 110
Tatum, Mrs. (Bonanza) 68
Thomas, Laura (Johnny Ringo)
    41
Thompson, Mrs. (Streets of
    San Francisco) 66
Thompson, Doug (Streets of
    San Francisco) 66
Tony (I Dream of Jeannie) 98,
    100
Townsend, Charles (Charlie's
    Angels) 177